Murder, Rape, and Treason

Judicial Combats in the Late Middle Ages

DEEDS OF ARMS SERIES

Series Editor: Steven Muhlberger, Nipissing University

This series of source readers makes available to a broad audience original accounts of famous displays of martial and chivalric prowess from the Middle Ages and early Renaissance. The books provide short, vivid introductions to particular topics and events, and can also be used in combination to look at the complex phenomenon of chivalric competition. Each volume includes a comprehensive introduction, color gallery of contemporary illustrations, and bibliography for further reading. Five volumes are currently scheduled for publication; others are under consideration.

Check our website for updates: www.freelanceacademypress.com.

DEEDS OF ARMS SERIES   VOLUME 5

Murder, Rape, and Treason

Judicial Combats in the Late Middle Ages

by Steven Muhlberger and Will McLean

Freelance Academy Press, Inc.
www.FreelanceAcademyPress.com

On cover: A combatant pins his opponent to the ground to finish him with a dagger thrust. (c. 1430)
(Source: MS U860.F46 1450, 42v, Yale Center for British Art in New Haven, Connecticut)
A fencing manual (Fechtbüch) from the early 15th century, Glaidatoria's emphasis is on the judicial duel,
and the same grim finishing blows it shows delivered with the dagger are both found in contemporary artistic
depictions and literary accounts of actual duels.

Freelance Academy Press, Inc., Wheaton, IL 60189
www.freelanceacademypress.com

Printed in the United States of America
by Publishers' Graphics

ISBN 978-1-937439-41-5

Library of Congress Control Number: 2019947123

Contents

Preface

Remembering Will McLean

In my role as editor of the Deeds of Arms series, I wanted Will McLean, amateur scholar and reenactor extraordinaire, to write this book. Unfortunately, Will died at an early age, soon after I proposed that the two of us should collaborate on this volume. He had indicated an interest in the project but the progress of his disease prevented us from planning or writing or even communicating during the last weeks of his life. He and I had worked together before, on the history of formal combats in the late Middle Ages, and I think such a collaboration would have been both productive and a lot of fun. As it is, I wish to acknowledge his work in this area by listing him as co-author of *Murder, Rape, and Treason*. Primary responsibility for the final form of the book is, of course, mine.

Will McLean was not an academically trained historian, but his intelligence and talent for serious research were remarkable. In the 1970s he joined the Society for Creative Anachronism (SCA), and soon became a serious reenactor of later medieval society. When he investigated a subject, his logic and use of documentation was first rate. He published a number of articles, mainly on the re-creation of medieval combat, and, with Jeffrey Forgeng, a short book, *Daily Life in Chaucer's England*, a more general guide to re-creating Will's favorite historical period, the late fourteenth century. *Daily Life* came out of a crucial time in the history of medieval re-creation in North America, when many people who had become dissatisfied with the rather loose standards of the SCA – the largest medieval re-creation organization – were revisiting the source material that might provide a better foundation for a more authentic re-creation. Will's research was among the best produced by this community of stricter re-enactors. Will also contributed to this movement by his personal example as a participant in the in-costume activities and as a designer and organizer of more focused re-enactments.

The research most relevant to *Murder, Rape, and Treason* was Will's re-investigation of how one might devise a better method of combat for re-creating late medieval tournaments. The founders of the SCA had come up with a very simple style of "counting blows." Solid ("killing") blows with rattan weapons to the head or the body resulted in "death," while similar blows to the arms or upper legs meant that the struck warrior could not use the affected limb for the rest of the fight. This system had the advantage of simplicity, but it was not based on a thorough knowledge of human anatomy, the effectiveness of medieval armor, or how medieval jousters or tourneyers determined victory in the lists. In 1994, Will devised different methods of assigning victory and defeat in a deed of arms, based mainly on medieval accounts of what happened in various combats. His reconstructions of armored combat and his re-creations of the formats of late medieval deeds of arms, described in his articles, "Running a Tournament by King René's Rules" and "A New Way to Get Maimed," became very influential among people who wanted to experience events modelled more on medieval practice than on modern elimination sports tournaments.

In the 2000s Will continued to write on practical and elegant methods of re-creation; much of this material was made available in his blog, *A Commonplace Book*. In this period his most important contribution to martial arts re-creation was an article published in the *Journal of Medieval Military History*, "Outrance and Plaisance," on the meaning of those terms as descriptors of a formal deed of arms. Before this publication, it was generally accepted that a combat à outrance was a combat with sharp weapons, and a combat à plaisance was with blunted weapons. Will's article is a fine investigation of the actual usage of these words, which reveals much about contemporary attitudes of the men at arms who fought such combats. He demonstrated that it was not the weapons used that made a deed of arms à outrance, but the limits on the violence agreed to before the combat. Combat à outrance (to extremities), was combat that continued until one warrior or one team was either killed or captured.

I would love to say more about Will McLean, a notably kind, witty, humorous, and analytical companion, but I doubt I saw him in person more than a couple dozen times. He and I interacted primarily on paper or through the Internet. I deplored the distance between us when he was healthy and I found the unexpected onset of his illness to be entirely unfair, absurd and as commonplace as that sentiment always is. Perhaps somebody who knew him better will take up the task of writing a just portrait of a remarkable man. Until then we have an obituary at Legacy.com /The Daily Local (see Bibliography) that preserves some of the basic facts of his life.

The structure of this book is somewhat different from others in the Deeds of Arms series. Each section of the book alternates between my own discussion of judicial combats, which draws heavily from insights and analyses from Will McLean's writings on the subject, and source material in translation, which illustrates the formal structure and actual performance of judicial combats.

Steven Muhlberger

1.

Introduction

Deeds of arms – formal, limited combats – were an important part of late medieval warrior culture. In such structured events, warriors were able to display their identities and establish their worth as good men at arms before an audience that included their peers (or companions), their lords and captains, and the ladies who inspired them. Among the most interesting and prominent deeds of arms were the judicial duels that were characteristic of the late Middle Ages (14th and 15th centuries).

Before we go further, we must discuss terminology and distinguish between judicial duels (or judicial combats) and trial by battle. Trial by battle was an elaborate legal procedure that began with someone charging another with a crime. This accusation was called an "appeal" and initiating an appeal was called a pledge or wager of battle. The trial by battle or pledge of battle ideally ended with the accused and the accuser (or their champions) fighting to establish guilt or innocence in what is now called "judicial combat" or "judicial duel."

In previous eras, the trial by battle had been a fairly routine part of law enforcement in many European regions. By the second half of the 13th century however, such trials were increasingly restricted in their application. They were used to adjudicate guilt for a small number of very important capital crimes such as murder, rape, and treason. Trials took place mainly between military men of rank (men at arms) who were able to insist that their cause be decided by a judicial duel. This ability to insist that a judicial duel was an important noble privilege was necessary because stronger royal courts staffed by more professional judges were reluctant to allow the implicit claim that a duel represented a better justice than that dispensed by human judges.

In some periods, trials were fairly commonly available, although it was rare for the duels to be fought to a conclusion. It was possible for trials to be resolved peacefully by negotiated settlement or the decision of the judge. Because duels were rare, they attracted a lot of attention. The cases in which duels were approved were controversial in themselves, as was the legal procedure. Was the result of a judicial combat truly an expression of the will of God? Medieval lawyers and ordinary observers often had their doubts. The controversies surrounding duels resulted in a number of late medieval duels being written up in some detail. These duels are therefore among the best known medieval deeds of arms.

The word "duel" suggests to most people the conflicts over points of honor so vividly evoked by Alexandre Dumas in his novel *The Three Musketeers* (1844; depicting 1625–1628). Such "duels of honor" (which were fought by "gentlemen" in Europe and North America right up to the 20th century) were not the judicial duels of the Middle Ages. Duels of honor had no place in the judicial system, though they were tolerated by the authorities when they lacked the will or the leverage to prevent dueling or punish those who took part in them. Duels of honor asserted or defended the social status of the participants. It is indicative of aristocratic values in the early modern period that duelists were willing to defy the legal authorities to fight to the death over insults and affronts that did not have the status of crimes.

The earlier trials by combat likewise were concerned with issues of honor and shame, but they also were used to decide whether a given person was guilty of a crime. Legal issues in the early and central Middle Ages were seldom resolved by careful examination of evidence. Rather, both accusers and defendants (to use the modern terms) were judged by their status in the community. Appeals – accusations made by an "appellant" – were often rebutted by the oaths of

co-swearers, men who supported the cause of the defendant. In such procedures, the balance of power, and not the balance of evidence, decided the issue.

Similarly, disputes could be decided by ordeals, the most famous of which
are the ordeal of fire, the ordeal of hot water, and the ordeal of cold water. In all
cases, a person needing to prove his innocence or the justice of his cause was
required to put himself in peril by, for instance, being immersed in cold water
and coming out of the ordeal relatively unscathed. Such ordeals were often
under clerical supervision, involving blessings and other rituals performed by
the clergy. The ordeal was an appeal to God for his intervention in the natural
course of things, such as protecting the subject of the ordeal from being burned
by a hot iron, so that it would be clear which side of the dispute was in the right.

What we now call criminal and civil cases could both be decided by ordeals,
or more precisely, by legal procedures that might ultimately lead to someone
undergoing an ordeal. Trial by ordeal always involved much negotiation about
who was subject to the ordeal and what form it would take. Likewise, interpret-
ing the results of an ordeal could not avoid subjective judgment. How well, for
instance, was a burned hand healing? What judgment did the state of the hand
indicate? The uncertainty or ambiguity inherent in any kind of ordeal has led
scholars to note that all ordeals were to some degree an "ordeal by public opinion."

Trial by battle was also a form of "ordeal by public opinion," and involved a
great deal of legal maneuvering. One common maneuver was the use of champions, professional warriors, to fight the duel. It is obvious that not everyone
involved in a legal case that might lead to a duel wanted to take part personally.
Indeed, many of the earlier accounts of duels that we possess involved property
disputes in which one or both parties were monastic corporations. Monks or
other clerics were, in theory, absolved from bloody combat, yet they were as
a group extremely wealthy and had to take prudent measures to uphold their
rights. The drastic nature of the duel in the early Middle Ages inspired many dis-
putants to negotiate an alternative settlement rather than take part in the duel.

Judicial duels, like the other ordeals, were seen as a method of reaching a
verdict when other methods were unable to reach one. If evidence or testimony

was not clear or was rejected by participants in a legal case, one could always turn to God. At the very least, putting rivals or champions against each other would likely result in a clear verdict. But there was, in fact, no guarantee of clarity even in the case of the duel.

The earliest record of a trial by battle comes from the end of the 6th century and is preserved in Gregory of Tours' *Ten Books of Histories,* also referred to as *History of the Franks.* Gregory shows trials and the judicial combat in some detail. They took place in the post-Roman Burgundian kingdom, where (according to the Burgundian code) this form of trial had been available since the early 6th century.

An early medieval duel, Burgundy, 590. Gregory of Tours, *History*

While King Gunthram was hunting in the Vosges forest he found traces of the killing of a buffalo. And when he harshly demanded of the keeper of the forest who had dared to do this in the King's forest, the keeper named Chundo the King's chamberlain. Upon this he ordered Chundo to be arrested and taken to Chalon loaded with chains. And when the two were confronted with each other in the King's presence and Chundo said that he had never presumed to do what he was charged with, the King ordered a trial by battle. Then the chamberlain offered his nephew to engage in the fight in his place and both appeared on the field; the youth hurled his lance at the keeper of the forest and pierced his foot; and he presently fell on his back. The youth then drew the sword which hung from his belt but while he sought to cut his fallen adversary's throat he himself received a dagger thrust in the belly. Both fell dead. Seeing this Chundo started to run to Saint Marcellus's church. But the King shouted to seize him before he touched the sacred threshold and he was caught and tied to a stake and stoned. After this the King was very penitent at having shown himself so headlong in anger as to kill a man who was faithful and useful to him.

This incident was not necessarily a typical or ordinary duel (because it is the first recorded one, we can hardly be sure). Two important men of the Burgundian court were involved in a serious violation of royal privileges to hunt. One of them, Chundo, was accused of the crime by the other, an unnamed "keeper of the forest." King Gunthram felt it impossible to either accept or reject this accusation, and he required the truth of the matter to be established by a duel between Chundo and the nephew of the unnamed keeper. The use of sharp weapons indicated the desire of the King for a decisive result, but that eluded him. King Gunthram was dissatisfied by the result – the death of Chundo – and had the survivor killed. The impression conveyed by this account is not of a clean, effective appeal to God's judgment, but of erratic and disproportionate royal action. Indeed, Gregory is well known for his skepticism of earthly authority. This first recorded medieval duel is also notable for revealing how controversy, at this early date, could surround the duel. It is not at all clear, even though it had been established by inclusion in the Burgundian Code earlier in the 6th century, that judicial combat enjoyed a secure place in the legal practice of the early Burgundian kingdom that same century.

Nonetheless, some characteristics typical of later judicial duels are here. We see the use of the duel to determine the rights and wrongs and resolve a difficult legal dispute—the difficulty here being the conflicting claims of the opponents. Additionally, it was fought between men of roughly similar status (in this case, they were both royal officials), so that the dispute could not easily be settled simply by reference to their rank. The duel was regulated by royal authority; in this case, the role of judge was taken by the King himself. That he did a poor job of it does not take away from the fact that the dispute and the procedure used to resolve it were of more than usual importance. The duel was a dramatic event:

for observers on the spot, for Gregory, who chose to include it in his history, and for his readers. Finally, a champion was used to represent one of the rivals, an action that became common in later centuries.

One of the foremost scholars of the ordeal, Robert Bartlett, has argued that the Burgundian kingdom and Eastern Frankish territories were the original homeland of ordeals. He has traced the use of ordeals through most of northern Europe. Frankish domination of that region in the Carolingian period seems to have promoted the spread of these trials.

We have looked at judicial duels primarily as a type of ordeal. They can also be viewed as *war*, another legal procedure available to noble or gentle warriors, which was an alternate method of dispute settlement in which rivals avoided the courts of their superior lords. What we call war is generally seen as a right legitimately exercised by sovereign rulers. It was far more widely exercised in the early and central Middle Ages, a period of fragmentary authority. Beaumanoir's well-known compilation of customary law in the French province of Beauvaisis from 1283 discusses *guerre* as a kind of war waged by nobles against their neighbors with the backing of their lineages. In 1340, the connection between war and the duel was made clear by Edward III's declaration of war on France. Edward asserted his claim on France by appealing to "Our Lord Jesus Christ and our right" and offered to settle the dispute in a less destructive way than by open war: Edward proposed that he and Philip VI fight for the French crown by a one-on-one combat, or a combat of the two kings each accompanied by one hundred "of the most suitable people," or finally a pre-arranged battle at Tournai. These proposals, which like other efforts to limit warfare between Christians (or at least to be seen as doing so), have an obvious similarity to earlier medieval challenges and to the much more common smaller-scale duels.

The era of the central Middle Ages (c. 1000-1300), provides access to a large number of charters describing monastic properties and disputes about them. Because land was wealth and status and a firm resolution of a land dispute, in theory, would last forever, monasteries preserved their charters with great diligence. Charters, which recorded the resolution of the settlements, usually described the histories of the disputes in detail. Such disputes were often settled by trial by battle, although quite often without the case continuing to the stage of actual combat. Thus, the mass of monastic charters provides us with a huge archive illustrating how land law really worked, often through negotiation of a trial by battle, which could result in a duel, or in the avoidance of a duel through a compromise settlement.

The following charter from the 1060s illustrates how an appeal to judicial combat might never result in actual fighting. Two monasteries in the Paris region, Saint-Serge and Saint-Aubin, determinedly insisted on the rights over a patch of territory until "the dispute concerning this matter grew so great that the members of the household of each monastery were preparing to contend with staves and shields against each other concerning this matter." The abbot of Saint-Serge thought that a fight between monks would be an unheard-of evil and made a great and successful effort to find a peaceful solution. This charter can stand in for many disputes in which the opponents were determined to have their rights but were not so stubborn as to insist, foolishly, on fighting the duel if an alternative might produce a reasonably good settlement. One wonders about the statement that two monasteries were preparing for a large battle. Was this a real possibility?

Abbots Daibert and Otbrannus prevent a battle between their monks. France, 27 and 28 April, 1064 – charter

Concerning the concord made between the monks of Saint-Aubin and the monks of Saint-Serge concerning the weir of the mill of Varennes.

Let it be known to all faithful of the holy church of God, and especially to our successors, that a serious altercation arose between the monks of Saint-Serge [of Angers] and the monks of Saint-Aubin [of Angers] over the land to be used for the weir at the mill of

Varennes. The monks of Saint-Serge affirmed that ancient custom required that the weir be constructed from the [plot of] land placed in front of the mill. The monks of Saint-Aubin, however, did not want to concede that the land placed around the mill was to be used for building a weir. The dispute concerning this matter grew so great that the members of the household of each monastery were preparing to contend with staves and shields against each other concerning this matter. Such a turn of events disheartened Abbot Daibert of Saint-Serge beyond measure, especially since it might cause monks to want to fight against other monks. He [Abbot Daibert], employing the greatest supplication, sent word to Abbot Otbrannus of Saint-Aubin [to warn him] lest such an unheard-of evil as this occur and lest monks, who ought to show the example of concord and peace to others, become the cause of perdition.

The following charter of 1098, describing a conflict involving at least three French ecclesiastical communities – Holy Cross, Angles and Fontaines – shows a land dispute going all the way to a violent conclusion. Holy Cross seems to have controlled or claimed a marsh, while other institutions disputed those claims. All of those who felt aggrieved with Holy Cross combined their interests to put up a side in a judicial combat. Exactly what the terms of the alliance were is unclear. The combat was one man against another. It seems that there were enough duels in the region that there was a fixed location for them, an "area where champions habitually were led to decide such matters through judicial combat." And whereas in the earlier charter we have an abbot unhappy with conflict between monks, the authors of this charter showed no hesitation in rating their victory as a divine judgment representing true justice: they saw their judges, in this case, as God and Saint Martin and celebrated wholeheartedly.

Trouble between two monasteries leads to a judicial battle. France, 1098 – charter

Notice relating how the monks of Fontaines [a priory of St-Martin of Tours] recovered their marsh at Angles through the proof of a judicial battle held against the monks of Talmont.

Yet because their complaint about the gift was going nowhere, the monks approached Count William of Poitou, lamenting and promising [him] money so that he might make right to them concerning the monks of Talmont, who, relying on the gift of Pippin, were fraudulently keeping hold of the marsh at Angles.

He [the count] forthwith commanded the abbot of Holy Cross of Talmont to appear before him to answer [literally "to make right"] concerning this matter. And when the claims of both parties had been narrated before the count, Odo de Roches, at the request both of the count and of everyone else, judged that the monks of Saint Martin, according to the charter of prior donation which had been read out there, namely the donation made by the late William, ought to demonstrate through the approbation of judicial combat [*duellum*] that the marsh, concerning which such a great contention had arisen, had been given to Saint Martin and Saint John in the same [initial charter of] donation.

And then they came to Moutiers-les-Maufaits at the count's command to decide the issue between them through a judicial combat. Finally, the armed champions were both led to the church, where they both pronounced themselves ready to take the oath.

But the champion of Saint Martin, who agreed to go first in swearing the oath with his hand being held, swore to the aforesaid Odo the following oath so that all could hear: "When William the Youth of Talmont, about whom I am capable of speaking, gave the land of Fontaines and the land of Angles to Saint Martin and

Saint John in his charter and gift, he included the marsh in that gift." Then, truly, the other champion claimed that he had perjured himself with this oath.

When everyone hurried to reach the area where champions habitually were led to decide such matters through judicial combat, the canons of Angles came to Prior Ainulfus and the other monks of Fontaines, asking that they [the monks of Fontaines] include them in the trial by battle against the monks of Holy Cross. He [Ainulfus] freely agreed to their request, and not only accepted them jointly in this proof by combat but also accepted all others who were known to hold anything in that marsh.

And when the champions came together to do combat, the injustice [done by the monks of Holy Cross] did not remain in doubt for very long, but was quickly revealed by the lord. In fact, the champion of the monks of Holy Cross and their allies was shamefully defeated and laid low without delay, and he thus acquired nothing else for the monks of Holy Cross save the highest shame and the greatest harm. Weighed down with shame and sadness on account of this defeat, they [the monks of Holy Cross], weeping and overcome with sadness, departed along with those others who had wanted to seize the marsh belonging to Saint Martin. The monks of Fontaines and their champion, on the other hand, offering immense thanks to the most just judges, God and their patron saint, Saint Martin, returned quickly and joyfully to their house in order to take possession of their rights.

So that the truth of these things which are recorded above might be believed, not one but a large number of proper witnesses were introduced to strengthen the testimony of the truth.

Thus trial by battle was one method of deciding serious legal cases and seems to have been used for various purposes across Western Europe. Thanks to the rather full records of the English judiciary, we have quite a bit of information about the use of "approvers" in a variation of the judicial combat unique to England. If several people were accused of theft, it was possible for one of the accused to be granted leniency by agreeing to turn state's evidence. This might involve, and often did, the approver (the thief testifying for the Crown) fighting a judicial combat against his former friends. There was a routine that could involve the Crown providing weapons and even training for the approvers. If the approver won, he was not off the hook, but was allowed to leave the Kingdom rather than be hanged. This kind of judicial duel was not a prestigious public ceremony as we will see in later times, but simply a way of efficiently processing accusations of theft, which was a despised capital crime.

A curious example of how warfare, judicial dueling, and recreational combat might overlap can be found in the text of the *Song of My Cid (Cantar de mio Cid)*, dating from about 1200 and depicting people and events that supposedly took place in Spain about a century earlier. The duel takes place because the Carrión clan has seriously mistreated some of the women of El Cid. No legal penalty is specified but the gain or loss of honor is clear. The rights and wrongs of the case are to be resolved by a formal deed of arms, under the supervision of King don Alfonso and judges appointed by him. A field is marked out by barriers, and the rules of the engagement (which takes place on horseback) are that those who are chased out of the marked-off area lose. Is this a small battle, or a tournament? The structure of the event recalls the northern French tournaments of William Marshal's youth (the mid-12th century), but this is a far more serious competition, for the fates of kingdoms and noble clans are at stake. One wonders if this kind of judicial tournament (organized like a tournament, as a battle on horseback within boundaries) ever took place, or whether the drama inherent in noble competition for honor was best expressed in combat, or at least fictional accounts of combat.

Song of My Cid,
Castile, 12th-13th centuries – epic poem:

…Get up and go out to the field, infantes of Carrión,

it is time for you to fight like men,

the Campeador's men will not fail in anything.

If you come off the field well, you will have great honor,

if you are defeated, don't blame us,

for everyone knows that you went looking for it.-

Now the infantes of Carrión are repenting,

for what they did, they are filled with regret,

they wouldn't have done it for all there is in Carrión.

All three of the Campeador's men are armed,

King don Alfonso went over to see them,

the Campeador's men said,

-We kiss your hands as king and lord,

that you be field judge for them and for us,

help us fairly, allow no wrongs.

Here the infantes of Carrión have their band,

 we know not what they will plan or what they won't,

 in your hand our lord placed us,

protect our rights, for the love of the Creator.-

At that moment the King said, -With all my heart and soul.-

They bring them their horses, good ones and swift,

they blessed the saddles and mount confidently,

the shields that are well reinforced at their necks,

in their hands they take the shafts of the sharp lances,

these three lances have their own pennons,

and around them many mail men.

They now went out to the field where the markers were.

All three of the Campeador's men are in agreement

that each one of them should strike his adversary hard.

Behold at the other end the infantes of Carrión,

very well accompanied, for there are many relatives.

The King gave them judges to tell them what's right and what isn't,

that they not dispute with them about who is or isn't right.

When they were in the field King don Alfonso spoke,

-Hear what I say to you, infantes of Carrión,

this combat you might have had in Toledo, but you refused.

These three knights of my Cid the Campeador

I brought them safely to the lands of Carrión,

be in the right, don't commit any wrongs,

for whoever wishes to commit a wrong, I will severely prohibit it,

in all my kingdom he will not be welcome.-

Now it begins to grieve the infantes of Carrión.

The judges and the King point out the markers,

all those around them left the field,

they showed clearly to all six of them how they are laid out,

that there whoever went outside the marker would be defeated.

All the people cleared out around there,

that they not approach the markers by any more than six lance lengths.

They drew lots for field position, now they divided the sun equally,

the judges got out from between them, they are face to face,

then the Cid's men came at the infantes of Carrión

and the infantes of Carrión at the Campeador's men,

each one of them concentrates on his target.

They clasp their shields before their hearts,

they lower their lances along with the pennons,

they lower their faces over the saddlebows,

they struck their horses with their spurs,

the ground shook where they were riding.

Each one of them has his mind on his target,

all three on three have now come together,

those that are nearby think that at that moment they will fall dead.

Pedro Bermúdez, he who challenged first,

met with Fernán González face to face,

they strike each other's shield fearlessly.

Fernán González pierced the shield of Pedro Bermúdez,

he hit only air, he did not strike flesh,

in two places his lance shaft broke cleanly apart.

Pedro Bermúdez remained steady, he did lose his balance from it,

he received one blow, but he dealt another,

he broke the boss of the shield, he split it in two,

he went through it entirely, it didn't protect him at all,

he stuck his lance into his chest, it didn't protect him at all.

Fernando wore three layers of mail, this helped him,

two of them broke on him and the third held up,

the padded tunic with the shirt and with the mail

out from his mouth the blood came, his saddle-girths broke,

not one of them was of any use to him,

over the croup of the horse he was thrown to the ground.

In this way the people thought he is fatally wounded.

The other dropped the lance and the sword he took in hand,

when Fernán González saw it, he recognized Tizón,

rather than wait for the blow he said, -I am defeated.-

The judges granted it, Pedro Bermúdez let him be.

Martín Antolínez and Diego González struck each other with their lances,

the blows were such that both lances broke.

Martín Antolínez took his sword in hand, it

lights up all the field, it is so clean and bright,

he gave him a blow, he hit him a glancing blow,

it broke away the top of the helmet,

it cut away all the helmet straps,

it tore off the mailed hood, and reached the coif,

the coif and the hood all were ripped away,

it cut the hairs on his head, and it reached well into the flesh,

one part fell to the ground and the other remained.

When precious Colada has struck this blow,

Diego González saw that he would not escape with his soul,

he turned his horse to face his opponent.

At that moment Martín Antolínez hit him with his sword,

he struck him broadside, with the cutting edge he did not hit him.

Diego González has sword in hand, but he does not

use it, at that moment the infante began to shout,

-Help me, God, glorious lord, and protect me from this sword!-

He reined in his horse and, dodging the sword,

rode it outside the marker, Martín Antolínez remained on the field.

Then said the King, -Come join my company,

by all you have done, you have won this battle.-

The judges grant it, that he says the truth.

Both men have won, I'll tell you of Muño Gustioz,

how he fared against Asur González.

They strike each other on their shields with such great blows,

Asur González, rugged and valiant,

struck the shield of don Muño Gustioz,

through the shield he broke his armor,

the lance hit only air, for it did not strike flesh.

This blow struck, Muño Gustioz struck another one,

through the shield he broke his armor,

he broke through the shield's boss,

it could not protect him, he broke through his armor,

he hit him on one side, not near the heart,

he thrust his lance and the pennon right through his flesh,

pushing it through the other side an arm's length,

he gave it a twist, he tipped him from the saddle,

when he pulled back on the lance he threw him to the ground,

the shaft came out red as did the lance-tip and the pennon.

Everyone thinks that he is mortally wounded.

He repositioned his lance and halted over him, said Gonzalo Ansúrez,

-Don't strike him, for God's sake! He is defeated since this is finished.-

Said the judges, -This we hear.-

The good king don Alfonso ordered the field cleared,

the arms that remained there he took them.

The Campeador's men left fully honored,

they won this combat, thanks to the Creator.

Great is the grief through the lands of Carrión.

The King sent my Cid's men at night,

so that they not be attacked or have fear.

Like prudent men they ride day and night,

behold them in Valencia with my Cid the Campeador,

they left the infantes of Carrión in disgrace,

they have fulfilled their duty that their lord demanded of them,

my Cid the Campeador was pleased by this.

Great is the shame of the infantes of Carrión,

 whoever scorns a good lady and then abandons her

may such befall him or even worse.

2.

Limitations on the use of judicial combats

Although trial by battle and judicial combats were widely used in the first Christian millennium in Europe (as were other ordeals), some observers always doubted the legitimacy of such procedures. Most ordeals involved clerical supervision and the blessing of various instruments or persons, presumably to make the decision authorized by the ordeal more legitimate. This appeal to divine power and justice made sense to many people, as God was the ultimate source of all justice, and the appeal to divine intervention was just a specialized case of what was done all the time. Others thought that the appeal to God in an ordeal was an attempt to force God's hand, or "tempt God," a dubious procedure at best. As the clergy of Western Europe began to see themselves and their institutions as more strictly separated from those of the lay world, theologians and canon lawyers began to turn against the ordeal. Those skeptical of the ordeal came to be repelled by the fact that justice was all too often dispensed by rough people with bloody hands. By the beginning of the 13th century, ecclesiastical authorities had come to a near consensus that clerics should not be involved in any kind of legal prosecution that might result in blood or death. That blood was an important issue is made clear by Canon 18 of the Fourth Lateran Council of

1215, in which there is a rule stating that the shedding of blood during surgery was considered almost as egregious as presiding over court cases that might lead to execution of the guilty. The Council was a turning point for this issue and for many others. In relatively short order, clerics withdrew their participation in trials by ordeal.

Canon 18 of the Fourth Lateran Council, Rome, 1215 – ecclesiastical legislation

SUMMARY. Clerics may neither pronounce nor execute a sentence of death. Nor may they act as judges in extreme criminal cases, or take part in matters connected with judicial tests and ordeals.

TEXT. No cleric may pronounce a sentence of death, or execute such a sentence, or be present at its execution. If anyone in consequence of this prohibition (*hujusmodi occasions statuti*) should presume to inflict damage on churches or injury on ecclesiastical persons, let him be restrained by ecclesiastical censure. Nor may any cleric write or dictate letters destined for the execution of such a sentence. Wherefore, in the chanceries of the princes let this matter be committed to laymen and not to clerics. Neither may a cleric act as judge in the case of the Rotarii, archers, or other men of this kind devoted to the shedding of blood. No subdeacon, deacon, or priest shall practice that part of surgery involving burning and cutting. Neither shall anyone in judicial tests or ordeals by hot or cold water or hot iron bestow any blessing; the earlier prohibitions in regard to dueling remain in force.

The Lateran ruling did not bring trial by battle to an end, however. For a long time thereafter, clerical critics had to make arguments against the legitimacy of judicial duels. In the *Tree of Battles*, a treatise on the laws of war from the late 14th century, the French academic lawyer Honoré Bouvet, following the Italian professor and politician Giovanni da Legnano, argued that every major learned tradition of law rejected wager of battle. But Bouvet had to admit that Lombard law in Northern Italy allowed judicial combat in connection with certain major crimes, mostly secret or treasonous crimes, or those involving deceitful attacks on members of one's own family. Yet Bouvet's treatise also hints that despite the disapproval of clerical, university-trained lawyers, matters arising out of treachery as well as some rather humdrum property crimes were, under Lombard (regional) law, able to be settled by judicial combat.

Tree of Battles (L'Arbre de Batailles) by Honoré Bouvet, France, 1387 – legal treatise

CXI

That to give wager of battle is a thing condemned.

Now let us return to the other part of my subject in which I spoke of one man appealing another by wager of battle; for this is a very subtle matter, so that clerks and nobles are often in great doubt about it. I wish, so far as I can, to enquire into all the cases in which the law allows wager of battle to be given.

But before I name them I wish to show plainly how according to divine law, the law of nations, the law of decretals, and civil law, to give wager of battle and to receive it for the purpose combat is a thing reproved, and is condemned by reason. I say, first of all, it is a thing condemned according to divine law, for the Holy Scripture condemns everything by which we tempt God our lord; but in doing this we tempt him, for we wish to know if God will help him who is in the right, and certainly to ascertain the will of God by experiment is an unworthy thing, and divine law does not allow it. And I can prove again that it is tempting God. We say that to ask for anything against nature is to ask a miracle, or to tempt God;

but it is against nature that the weak should conquer the stronger, yet we see that, in the hope that God would help him, a weak man offers wager of battle to a strong man. Clearly this is to tempt God…

CXII

Concerning the cases in which it is permissible to give wager of battle.

Now, although we have seen that wager of battle is a thing reproved by law, for the reason that worldly customs and usages have ordained the contrary I pray you to allow us to consider the cases in which law allows and suffers such battle to be made. And I tell you that there are few of them,…

…We have certain laws which are extraordinary, that we call the Lombard laws, and therein are several cases in which wager of battle, followed by combat in the lists, can be given; and for this reason we must consider all the cases found therein.

The first case of wager of battle according to Lombard law;

The first case is reasonable enough, in my opinion, considering the nature of this action; for if a man accuses another of having designed to kill the King, or of having designed to give orders to have him killed or poisoned, and the other says that this not true and appeals to battle, his adversary is obliged to answer and to appoint a day.

The second case… Another case in which Lombard law allows wager of battle is the following: if the husband accuses his wife having plotted his death evilly, either secretly by poison, or by other means, and one of her relations comes forward saying that is not true, and wishes to defend this suit against the husband, Lombard law says that he should be heard.

[3] There is further indication which this Lombard law allows wager of battle: that is, when a man has killed another secretly during a truce, and wishes to prove by his body that he has done this in self-defense, the Lombard law ordains that he shall be heard.

[4] Again, another law, speaking without distinction of peace or war or truce, in the case of any homicide committed secretly wager can be given, and the accused can prove his innocence by his body.

[5] There is, again, another case. If a man has the right of succession after the death of one of his relations, and kills him secretly, and is accused of it by another, and by his body is willing to prove the contrary, he is permitted according to Lombard law to defend himself.

[6] Then follows another case in which the Lombard law allows wager of battle. If a man has a serf, and the serf is accused of larceny, and the fact cannot be proved, then if the lord wishes to defend this accusation and prove the innocence of the serf by his body, the Lombard law says that he should be heard.

[7] Next another case is given. If a man is accused of having committed the sin of adultery with a married woman, and wishes to defend himself, Lombard law allows wager.

[8] That said law has also ordained another case. If a man accuses a woman of the sin of adultery committed secretly, and the husband, or one of his friends, or any champion, wishes to defend her with his body, he must be heard. And it appears that this law speaks more especially of a woman has never had a husband.

[9] Some speak further of another case which seems to me against reason and against all laws, namely: if a man has possessed or held a movable thing, or an immovable, for the space of thirty years, and another accuses him of having obtained it by false pretenses and wishes to prove it by his body, he must be heard. But I say, even supposing that this law does ordain thus, that if he who has prescriptive [customary] right replies to the other: "My dear friend, what you say does not concern me," I ask you whether he ought to be obliged to accept this gage (=pledge, wager), for it seems to me that he is not so obliged, seeing that right by prescription [=

custom, long use] is accepted everywhere.

[10] Now the Lombard law speaks of another case. If two men have a dispute and one of them produces witnesses to prove his claim, and the other produces the same witnesses, and if, after these have given evidence for the first time their evidence is found to vary, and one of these witnesses wishes to offer wager to the other, Lombard law permits battle.

[11] Then there is another case according to the same Lombard law: if a man demands a thousand francs from another, saying that the father of that other, from whom he inherits his goods, owed them to him; if the son denies this, and a man has no other proof, but wishes to prove it by his body, the law decides that he should be heard.

[12] Another case in which Lombard law permits battle is this: if a man accuses another of having secretly set fire to a house, or a barn, or a village, and wishes to prove it by his body and if the other maintains the contrary and wishes to defend himself, the Lombard law allows this battle.

[13] I speak further of another case. If a husband, to gain his wife's dowry, accuses her of adultery, and her brother, or one of her relations, or a champion, wishes to defend her, and the sin is not patent, in this the Lombard law allows wager.

[14] I must speak, further, of another case according to the said law; the case of a man who accuses another of having laid hands on his wife villainously, or with the intention of villainy.

[15] There is also another case: that if a man wishes to accuse another of having falsely perjured himself, the latter may defend himself by his body.

[16] Another case: if a man maintains that he has been in possession of a certain thing and another has dispossessed him of it evilly, then if the latter denies this the law allows battle. And I understand the law to this effect, that when he who has possession wishes to

defend his claim, or says: "you say that you had possession first and that I have dispossessed you wrongly, and I say the contrary, and that I held first as my inheritance, and you have dispossessed me wrongly," then law allows battle.

And although some doctors in this matter put forward other cases which are not clearly explained, I pass them by for the present, for later I wish to make several statements under this head.

After 1215, and perhaps before, judicial combats were not seen as depending on the blessings and supervision of clerical judges. It was more a right and duty of armed men than a ritual supervised by the clergy. Warriors maintained their status in society by their willingness and ability to defend their rights by fighting. Trials by battle thus continued. But during the 13th century some lay lords, no doubt influenced by clerical authorities and professional, learned judges, began to restrict the use of judicial combats. These restrictions were partly motivated by the desire of greater lords with superior jurisdiction to direct more cases into their own courts. One of the most important of such lords was King Louis IX of France, a man known for both personal piety and his desire to encourage and enforce what he considered the best standards of Christian behavior, a man who often worked on the advice of Franciscan and Dominican friars, who were, in the 13th century, on the cutting edge of ecclesiastical reform. Louis' prestige was such that he succeeded in implementing a number of reforms, including forbidding judicial combats in the areas under his jurisdiction. In 1258, Louis was able to abolish trial by battle for the rest of his reign. His immediate successors were not able to maintain that position against the pushback from those of his lords who enjoyed rights of high justice (including the right to adjudge trial by battle) and from important urban communities which enjoyed the same privilege. Eventually, however, a compromise was reached which regulated the use of trial by battle and the format of judicial combats, which we can see in Philip IV's ordinance of 1306.

In this ordinance document, at first glance, it might seem that the aristocrats

who upheld judicial combats had won concessions from Philip IV, as the ordinance acknowledged that trial by battle had a place in the legal system of
France. A closer examination reveals a near-total victory for royal power and
royal control of judicial combat. Here at the beginning of the 14th century we
are far from the situation seen in the 11th century during which property disputes might be settled by combat on a fairly routine basis. The judicial combats
authorized by the ordinance were monopolized by the royal judicial system and
restricted to a very few extremely serious crimes with an element of treachery:
treason, murder, and rape (but not larceny). Even for these crimes duels were
allowed only when guilt could not be resolved in other ways. Judicial combats
under Philip's ordinance were defined in great detail. They were elaborate per-
formances which by their complexity alone would be and could be used only
in the most important cases, when the royal authorities felt that the individual
case justified the vast amount of preparation required. Judicial duels were, in
fact, seldom used in France. It is worth noting that in England at the same
time, where combats were not so rare and not so prestigious, there was also a
reduction in the number of combats.

3.

Ordinances regulating judicial combats from the 14th century

If the measure of judicial combats is their routine nature and number, the 14th century could be seen as an era of decline. But if we consider the prestige associated with such combats, it might be regarded as a golden age for duels. The 14th century saw the first half of the Hundred Years War and similar conflicts elsewhere in Europe. This led to great increase in the number of free men who were used to enforcing their rights, defending their property, or proving their status by the use of arms. The diplomacy and warfare of the entire era was dominated by the claims of Edward III to the throne of France. Edward's claims (1340) were stated in a semi-legal form and emphasized the importance of God's judgment. Like kings, lesser men of a military background felt that their pride and status were closely identified with their ability to defend themselves. Similarly, political disputes could be visualized as either war or criminal activity. For instance, treason was considered the ultimate crime, the ultimate betrayal, which should be punished according to the model of war.

Duels between noble rivals may or may not have been less common in the 14th century, but they seem to have been better documented, both in chronicle accounts and in formal documents meant to regulate the practice. Philip IV's ordinance of 1306 provided the most elaborate model for late medieval judicial duels. It's quite clear that one of the motives for this ordinance was to ensure royal control of such duels. Likewise, the duels so carefully designed were meant to resolve disputes between men at arms—in other words, professional warriors who very likely were gentlemen. Similar ordinances were enacted in other jurisdictions. The ordinances were created not only for these purposes, but also to guarantee as often as possible that the combatants in such a duel would be on an even footing in regard to harness and other preparations.

The ordinance reveals a number of characteristics of trial by battle in the early 14th century. Such trials were treated as matters of the greatest importance. They were associated with the highest authority in the realm, the King. They were only appropriate for very serious crimes (murder, rape, and treason), and even then, only when guilt or innocence could not be otherwise determined. The legal procedures specified in the ordinance are very specific and include a great deal of petitioning and documentation justifying the "appeal" by one party against another.

The use of oaths was an important characteristic of the procedure. Trial by battle may not have been under clerical supervision or jurisdiction, but it did share in the religious ritual that flavored all important agreements. The ordinance provided a script for those taking part, and also specifies the equipment, setting, actions and gestures of the two parties. It is clear that such a procedure was not likely to be routine, nor could it be seen as suitable for everybody. In particular, the weapons and armor used in a trial under the terms of the ordinance were those associated with gentlemen—in other words, the military class. The role of personal or family honor was also very important. The procedure is not identified as a "duel," but as a gage, a "pledge" or "wager" of battle, in which a warrior of standing (or perhaps a champion) committed himself, his body and his honor to ensuring that justice was done.

Ordinance of Philip IV, France, 1306 – royal legislation

The following are the ceremonies and ordinances which pertain to pledge of battle resolved by conflict. According to the Constitutions established by the good King Philip of France.

Philip by the grace of God King of France, to all those who will see these present letters, greetings.

Knowing that formerly for the common profit of our realm, we would have forbidden generally to all our subjects all manner of wars and all pledges of battles; by which many malefactors have advanced themselves by the strength of their bodies and false tricks, to do homicides, treasons, and all sorts of evils, wrongs and excesses, because when they have done them covertly and in secret, they are not able to be convicted by any testimony, and so the crime goes unpunished. And because what we did was for the common profit and safety of our realm: in order to suppress the cause of evil in said evildoers, we have our above said prohibition moderated, by this in which it appears evidently that homicide or treason or other wrongs, evils, or acts of violence (excepting larceny), have been done, covertly or secretly, for which capital punishment of death ought to follow, so that he who has done it cannot be convicted by testimony or other sufficient manner: We desire that in default of another point, that or those who by circumstantial evidence or presumptions resembling the truth for having this deed, have been suspected of such deeds, appeal [accuse] and summon to pledge of battle: and we suffer in these cases the pledge of battle to take place. And because for this justice only we moderate our aforesaid prohibition in places and in terms in which the pledge of battle should not have taken place before our said prohibition. For this was not at all our intention that this prohibition ought to be repealed nor moderated in any case before or after the date of our present letters; of which condemnations, absolutions or inquests ought to be done, so that one should be able to judge them, absolve them or condemn them as the case requires and is clearly fitting. And in the testimony of this We have had these letters sealed with our great seal. Given at Paris on Wednesday after Trinity 1306.

II. Note the four things which ought to appertain before *gage* [pledge] of battle ought to be adjudged.

And first we wish and ordain that it should be a notorious thing, certain and evident, that the crime has taken place; and that is what is meant by the clause above where it says homicide, treason or other similar evil by evident presumption, etc.

The second is that the case ought to be such that natural death ought to follow from it, except in the case of larceny, which gage does not fall under; and this is the clause from which the penalty of death ought to follow.

The third is that nothing can be punished otherwise than by way of pledge; and this is the clause on secret treason, so that the one who has done it is not able to defend himself but by his body.

Fourth, that the one who wishes to appeal should decry the deed by clues or evident presumption; and this is the clause of evidence.

II. That the defendant ought to come to present himself before the judge without delay.

Note that in pledge of battle every man who says the truth for the sake of honesty ought to surrender himself and present himself without adjournment if he knows it; but he is allowed a good delay so that he can have his friends. And if he doesn't come without an adjournment, truly for this his right is diminished nor his honor advanced.

Likewise we wish and ordain according to the text of our letters that although larceny should incur the penalty of death, however larceny does not fall under pledge of battle, just as it is contained in the clause of larceny; except, et cetera.

III. How the appellant proposes his case before the judge of the appeal.

Likewise we wish and order that when one proposes any case of pledge of battle from which penalty of death ought to ensue as it is said, excepting larceny, it suffices that the appellant says that he appeals to make or cause to make the case by himself or by another, supposing that the appellant does not name him.

Likewise if the case is proposed in general terms as to say: I [name] say and wish to say, maintain and sustain that he, [name of accused] has traitorously killed or made [name of another accused] to kill someone else, we wish and ordain that this proposition ought not to suffice and should be unworthy of a response, according to the customary procedure of our court of France; but it is fitting to him to declare the place where the crime was committed, the time and the day, the person killed or betrayed. However, in this condition there should be information of the crime, which would not of course need to say the hour nor the day which can be too secret to know.

Likewise we wish and ordain that if someone adjudges a combat contrary to the customs contained in our said letters, all which will be done to the contrary will be recalled and revoked.

Likewise we wish and ordain that the plaintiff or appellant ought to say or have an advocate make his argument before us or his judge competent against his opposing party, him being present. And he ought to hold back from saying something evil which serves only his side of the quarrel; and he ought to conclude and require that if the accuser or the defendant confesses that the things put forward by him are true, that he ought to be condemned to be forfeited, and his body and goods confiscated to Us, or to be punished by such

penalty as law and custom and the matter requires. And if the said
appellee or defendant denies it, then the said appellant ought to say
that he is not able to prove through testimony nor otherwise than
by his body against his or by his advocate, in the closed field as a
gentleman and prudhomme ought to do, in our presence as their
judge and sovereign prince. And then he ought to throw his pledge
of battle; and then make up his retinue of the council of arms, of
horses and of all other things necessary and suitable to a pledge of
battle; and that in such a case, according to the nobility and condition which pertains to him, with all the petitions which ensue;
and these petitions, appellations and ordinance will be registered
to judge if he should have pledge or not.

And first he will say:

"Most excellent and puissant prince, and our sovereign lord;"
or if they are not of the realm of France, in place of sovereign lord
they should say: "And our judge competent, for to give a very brief
conclusion to the things which I have said, I protest and maintain
that by legal excuse of my body, I am able to have a gentleman for
my advocate this day, who in my presence if I am able, or in my
absence with the aid of God and Our Lady, will do his loyal duty to
my risks, costs and expenses, as is reasonable, whenever and however many times which he will plead to you; and similarly of arms
and of horses as my proper person, and so as to this case pertains."

Likewise we wish and ordain that the defendant, if he wishes,
should be able to speak to the contrary on his injustices, and require
the injuries said to him by the appellant to be compensated by such
a fine and penalty that he ought to bear if he has done the things
above said, and that the said appellant, saving the honor of Our
Majesty or of his judge competent, has falsely and evilly lied, and
as false and evil which he is to say of this; and if in defending with
the aid of God and of Our Lady, by his body or of his champion,

ceasing all legal excuse or delay, if he has said and judged that pledge of battle ought to be there, on the occasion, day and place which we, as their sovereign and true judge will ordain. And then he ought to take and pick up the pledge from the ground, and then make his aforesaid petitions, and require his advocate in case of legal delay or excuse to demand and retain the aid of arms and horses, and of all other things necessary and suitable to pledge of battle, according to his nobility and condition; and the surplus as well as is said. We wish and ordain that the words and defenses above said similarly be written and registered to know if he will have pledge or not, and for one compensating the other as justice requires. And for this each of them will swear, promise and oblige himself to appear at the day, hour and place assigned to them: as to the day, to know if the pledge will be there; as to the battle, if battle will take place there, according to the information of their process, which will be well viewed and reasonably regarded by notable and honorable clerics, knights and esquires, without favor to anyone: whether the pledge or not will be adjudged before them on the day and place, as it is said; on the penalty to the one who is at fault for being reputed recreant and convicted. And further we wish that those who do not give good and sufficient pledges are not to depart without our permission and will be arrested.

IV. How one of the parties departs without permission and is taken.

Likewise we wish and ordain that if either of the parties leaves without permission from our court after the pledges are thrown and received, we wish and ordain that the one who departs ought to be held and pronounced convicted and recreant.

Likewise, and because it is the custom that the appellant and the defendant enter the field carrying with them all the armor with which they intend to attack each other and defend themselves, leaving from their hotel on horseback, them and their covered horses and tunics and equipment of their arms; the visors lowered, the shields at the neck, glaives in hand, swords and belted dagger, and in all estates and manners which they intend to combat them, either on foot or on horseback. For if they make others carry their armor and they should carry their visors raised without our permission, or that of their judge, this to them should carry such prejudice that they should be compelled to combat in the state which they are able to enter the field, according to the present custom. And this custom appears to us in no way to be wearisome for the combatants, for our said letters and present chapters, we moderate and wish and ordain that the said combatants are able to leave in time, mount and arm as it is said, with the visors raised, making to carry before them their shields and their glaives and all other arms reasonable for fighting in such case. And as more than for having recognition of being true Christians, leaving their hotels, step by step, crossing themselves with their right hands, either carrying the crucifix or little banners on which are portrayed Our Lord and Our Lady, the Angels, and the Saints in which they have their faith and devotions; with the cross or banners, as is said, crossing themselves until they descend into their pavilions.

V. There follows the first of the three cries and the five defenses which the King of Arms or herald ought to make at all pledges of battle.

And first, the said King of Arms or herald ought to come on horseback to the gate of the lists, and there ought to cry once before the appellant comes.

Second, crying one more time, when the appellant and defendant have entered and have made their presentations to the judge and have gone down in their pavilions.

And third, when they are returned to make their final oaths, crying in the manner which follows in a loud voice:

"Attention, lords, knights, and squires and all manner of people, that our lord the King of France commands you and on penalty of loss of body and goods: that none should be armed, nor carry a sword, nor dagger nor other harness whatever, unless they are the guards of the field, and those who have permission for it from the King our lord.

"Again the King our lord commands and forbids that no one of whatever condition he might be, during the battle should be on horseback; the penalty for gentlemen being the loss of the horse, and for servitors the loss of the ear; and those who escort the combatants, descend from their horses who are at the gate of the field, will be required to send them on the said punishment.

"Further, the King our lord commands and forbids that anyone, of whatever condition he be, ought to enter the field, except for those who are deputed to be there for this; and they are not to be on the lists, on penalty of the loss of body and goods.

"Further, the King our lord commands and forbids everyone, of whatever condition he be, that he ought sit on bench or on the ground, so that each freely ought to be able to see the parties fight, on pain of losing a hand.

"Further, the King our lord commands and forbids that no one, whatever he may be, during the battle should speak, gesture, cough, nor spit, nor call out, nor do anything similar whatever he may be; and this on penalty of body and goods."

VI. How the appellant comes on horseback armed with all his weapons onto the field.

Likewise, and in accordance with the old customs of our realm of France the appellant ought to present himself in the field first and before the hour of noon, and the defendant before the hour of nones; and whosoever defaults on the hour, he is held and judged as convicted, if the mercy of the judge is not obtained; which customs we praise and approve, and which from now on should continue and hold good. However for some good reasons we are bestirred to modify the said ordinances, and consent that we or the judge is able to advance or delay the day or the hour according to the dispositions of the time, as it pleases all the judges; and take them in our hands for them to bestow and order to the honor and the good of both who can, or to give another day and hour, so much before the battle; and in them return to the same and similar point and situation as they have taken them, without being able ever to excuse, complain, forbid, nor protest, as their suitable judges.

VII. The petitions and protests which the parties make.

After this there follow the petitions and protests which the two parties are able to make at the entry of the listfield to the Constable, if the King has entrusted to him, and to the Marshals or Marshal whom they find there: to whom the appellant will speak or will have his advocate speak the words which follow, which is for many causes the best; and then those which he will say or will have said by his advocate similarly to the judge he will enter all on horseback. And first at the entry of the field:

"My very honorable lord Monseigneur the Constable, or Monseigneur the Marshal of the field; I am So-and-So [if he's speaking in person], or you see him there [if the advocate is making the speech] who is coming to present himself as you have ordered by our lord the King armed and mounted as a gentleman who ought to enter to fight against [name], over such a dispute, as the false and evil traitor or murderer that he is. And concerning this I call upon Our Lord, Our Lady and Monseigneur Saint George the good knight to be witnesses for those appointed by the King our lord on this day. And in order to accomplish this he [my client] has come and presents himself to do his duty. And he requests that you should deliver and apportion to him his section of the field, the wind, the sun and all which is necessary, profitable, and suitable in such a case. And this being done, he will do his true duty with the help of God, Our Lady and Monseigneur Saint George the good knight, as he is called; and protest that he is able to fight on horseback or afoot as may seem best to him, and to arm himself with his arms, or disarmed, and carry what he wishes as much for attacking as for defending at his pleasure, before fighting or during combat, if God gives him ability and strength to do it."

Likewise, that if his enemy [name] or his adversary carries other arms to the field which he ought not to carry by the constitution of France, that those are taken from him, and that in place of them he will have no others which he is not able to have.

Likewise, that if his enemy has arms forged by evil methods and spells, enchantments or invocations of enemies, by which it would be known that his good right would be hindered before the battle, in fighting, or after, that his good right and honor are not able to be diminished; rather ought the false and bad be punished as an enemy of God, traitor, or murderer, according to the condition of the case; and he ought to require that thereupon his said enemy ought to swear especially.

Likewise, he ought to require and protest that if by the will of God he has not by sunset defeated and vanquished his enemy, which he intends to do if it pleased God, however he should be able to require that it should be given to him as much of the day as would pass according to the rights and old customs; or otherwise he is able to protest if he has not the space of one day, which we to him must consent and grant.

Likewise, that in the case that [name] his adversary has not come at the required hour assigned by the King our lord, that he no longer be received but ought to be held to be reproved and convicted; the which petition is and will be at our liberty. However that if he is late without our will, that he will be thus as is said.

Likewise, he ought to ask and expressly petition that he should be able to carry with him bread, wine, and other viands to eat and drink over the space of a day if he should have need of it; and all other things suitable and necessary for him in such a case, both for him and his horse. Concerning which petitions and requests, both general and special, he ought to demand an official document. We wish and order that appellant or defendant is able to do the same, and in the said form. By which requests and petitions, if they are not especially forbidden to them, we wish and order that they are able to fight on horseback and armed on foot each as he wishes with all weapons and harness used to defend and attack, with the exception of all harness of evil trickery, charms, enchantments and invocations of the enemies, and all other things similarly forbidden to all good Christians, according to God and Holy Church.

VIII. How the lists and the stage of field arms are arranged, and the seat of the cross and the Te igitur, with the pavilions of the parties.

Likewise, we wish and order that all lists for the pledge of battle have six score feet of Tours in total; namely forty feet in width and eighty in length, which all the judges will make and maintain for the others who come. Likewise, we wish and order that the seat and pavilion of the appellant, whosoever he should be, will be at our right hand, and the right hand of his judge, and that of the defendant will be on the left.

IX. How each of the parties is to enter on horseback into the field before the judge and offer his case in writing.

Likewise, when each of them will have said, or had the things referred to by their advocates, before they will enter in the field they ought to lower their visors, and to enter with the visors lowered making the sign of the cross, just as is said. And in that state they ought to come before the stage where their judge will be, who will make them raise visors; and if the King is present the appellant ought to say to him:

"Most excellent and puissant prince, and our sovereign lord, I am [name], who is in your presence as you are our lawful lord and judge."

And if it is someone other than the King, he will say, "My most redoubtable lord, I am such, who in your presence as our competent judge, I have come at the day and hour which you have given to me, to do my duty against such and such, because of murder or treason which he has done; and concerning this I have taken God on my side, who will aid me today."

And when he will have said this or as close as he is able, a script will be given to him by his counsellors, which script will contain the words aforesaid, which he will offer to the Marshal from his own hand, who will receive it. And this being done we will give him permission to go down into his pavilion. And if it should be seen he does not know to say the aforesaid words, we wish and order that they ought to be in the office of the advocate.

Likewise, and after this the King of Arms or herald ought to climb on the gate of the lists and make his second cry and fifth defense in the form and manner which is said.

X. After this there follow the three oaths who done by those who wish to fight in pledge of battle.

Likewise, the appellant comes first, his visor raised, all on foot, leaving from this pavilion with the guards and counsel, armed with all his arms and armor, and his tunic underneath; and when he is under the stage where the judge is, he will kneel before a seat as richly adorned as it can be, where there will be the figure of our true

Savior and God Jesus Christ lying on the cross beneath a canopy, and to his right will be a priest, secular or regular, who to him will say in the following manner:

"Sir knight, or squire, or lord of such and such a place, you who are the appellant, you see here the truest remembrance of our Savior, the true God Jesus Christ, who wished to die and deliver his very precious body to death to save us. So to him you should petition for mercy and entreat him that on this day he will wish to aid you if you have the right; for he is the sovereign judge: remember the oaths which you have made, or otherwise your soul, your honor and you yourself are in peril."

Then the Marshal, when the speech is done, takes the appellant by his two hands together with the gauntlets, and puts the right hand on this cross and the left on the *Te igitur* [a prayer], and then says to him; "You, [name], you say it along with me." And he asks him if he has good right or if he wishes to perjure himself. And then the Marshal says: " I, such and such, appellant, swear on this remembrance of the Passion of Our Lord and Savior Jesus Christ and on the Holy Gospels which are here, and on the faith of the true Christian and of the holy baptism which I have from God, that I certainly have a good, just and holy quarrel and good right in this present pledge of battle and I appeal [such and such], as a false and evil traitor, or murderer, or man of false faith, as the case may be; which [adversary] has a very false and very evil cause and quarrel to defend. And this I will demonstrate to him today with my body against his, with the aid of God, Our Lady, and Monseigneur Saint George the good knight." Which oath being made, the said appellant should rise and return to his pavilion with those who have led him.

XI. How the defendant makes his first oath before the judge.

Likewise, after the guards come to the pavilion of the defendant they stay to make the oath in the form aforementioned, with his counsellors, armed with all his arms and the surplus. And when the priests well admonished him, the Marshal after all has been done and takes two hands together with his gauntlets, and puts them as he has done with those of the appellant. Then he says to him: "Such and such or lord of such a place, say as I say." And he asks if he has good right or if he wishes to perjure himself. And he says: "I so and so swear on this remembrance of the passion of Our Lord Jesus Christ, and the holy Gospels which are here, on the faith of a true Christian and on the holy Gospels which are here and the holy baptism to which I received from God that I have and believe firmly to have for certain good, holy and just quarrel and my good right to defend by this pledge of battle, against such and such who falsely and evilly has accused me as being false and evil, and this I will demonstrate today with my body with the help of God, our Lady, and Monseigneur Saint George the good knight." The oath having been made, said defendant should rise and return to his pavilion, just like the appellant.

Likewise, in the second oath the two parties come one after the other who (to abbreviate) likewise swear as said above.

XII. How the two parties, that is to say the appellant and the defendant, together make their final oaths before the judge.

Likewise, on the third oath the guards depart in each direction; they come in two parties, and lead them accompanied by the counsellors just as is said. They come step by step and side by side; and when they are kneeling before the cross and the *Te igitur*, the Marshal will take their right hands and remove the gauntlets from them, which he will place on the two arms of the cross; then there ought to be a priest present to call to mind the passion of our Lord God Jesus Christ, the perdition of the one who will have tort in soul and body, and the great oaths they have made and performed; the sentence of God, which is to aid the good right; them being consoled rather in the mercy of the prince, than in the ire and indignation of God and power of the enemy; which we order that should be the last of the three, for the mortal hate which is between them, especially when they see one another and hold together by the hands. Then the Marshal asks them, first to the appellant: "Do you, such and such, as appellant, wish to swear?" And if he repents and clears his conscience as a good Christian, we will detain him to our mercy or the judge's, before he has combatted, to give him penance or to order according to our pleasure; if it is so, we order that they are to be taken back to their pavilions, and from there they should not leave until our commandment or that of the judge whom they are before. And if they wish to swear and say yes, then the Marshal asks the defendant the same and then returns to the appellant and tells him to say as he does: "I, [name], appellant, swear on this true figure of the passion of our Lord God Jesus Christ, and on the holy Gospels which are here, on the faith of baptism which I hold as a Christian, on my true God, on the three sovereign joys of paradise, which I renounce for the three painful torments of hell, on my soul, my life, and my honor that I have good just and holy quarrel to combat this false and evil traitor, murderer, perjurer, and liar whom I see here before me; and concerning this I appeal to God as my true judge, Our Lady and Monseigneur Saint George the good knight. And therefore loyally, by the oaths which I have made, I do not intend to carry on myself or my horse words, stones, herbs, charms, enchantments, nor conjurations, invocations of the enemy, or any other thing where I have hope that is able to help me, nor to harm him. Nor do I have any recourse except in God and in my good right, by my body by my horse and by my arms. And then on this I kiss this True Cross and the holy Gospels, and am silent."

After the oaths are made the same Marshal goes to the defendant, and (to abbreviate) the one and the other say all just as is said.

And when the defendant has kissed the crucifix and the *Te igitur*, to clarify more the right to which he has, the Marshal takes them by the two right hands, and makes them hold them together. Then he tells the appellant that he say after him while speaking to his enemy: "Oh you, [name], whom I hold by the right hand, by the oaths which I have made, the cause of which I appealed you is true, by which I have good and loyal cause to accuse you, and on this day to combat you. You have a bad cause and no quarrel to combat and defend against me and you know it, of which I have appealed to God and Monseigneur Saint George the good knight to testify, as false traitor and liar which you are."

XIII. There follows the response of the defendant to the oath of the appellant, and how they return to their pavilions.

And after this the Marshal says to the defendant that he should speak after him while speaking to the appellant: "Oh you, [name], whom I hold by the right hand, by the oath which I have made, the cause for which you have appealed is false and evil, for which reason I have good and loyal cause to defend myself and combat against you this day. For you have an evil cause and no quarrel with me to appeal and combat against me, and you know it. From which from this I appeal to God, Our Lady and Monseigneur Saint George to testify, as false and evil as you are."

And after the oaths are all done and the words said, they ought to again kiss the crucifix and then each one together, fairly matched, rise and return to their pavilions to do their duty. And the priest then takes his cross and the *Te igitur*, and the seat on which they stand, removes himself and then retires. And the King of Arms or the herald, after all this, makes his cry in the form which is said.

XIV. There follows the last of the three cries.

Likewise, after this, which the King of Arms or heralds will have cried, and that one each will be seated and put in order without saying a word, and that the parties will be all prepared to do their duties then by the commandment of the Marshal, the said King of Arms or herald will come to the middle of the lists, to cry three times: "Do your duty." And at these words the two combatants will sally from their pavilions onto their stepladders to mount if they wish on their horses who will be there completely ready, and their weapons all around them, with which they ought to aid themselves, surrounded by their counsellors. And so their pavilions will quickly be removed from the lists and taken off the field.

XV. How the two parties are prepared outside of their pavilions to do their duty, at the cry of the Marshal who has thrown the gant (glove).

And when everything will be prepared the Marshal, who will be in the middle of the field and under the stands, takes the pledge in his hand and shouts three times saying: "Lessez-les aler, lessez-aler" [let them go]. Having said these words he throws the glove; and he who wishes quickly mounts the horse and he who does not wish pledge of battle ought to do according to his good pleasure. And their helpers depart without further ado, and leaving each his bottle of wine and a loaf in a napkin; and facing each other each does the best he can.

XVI. By what manner pledge of battle ought to be brought to an end, and how the victor drags the vanquished off the field.

Likewise we wish and ordain that pledge of battle should be concluded in one of two ways.

The first, when one of the parties confesses his guilt and surrenders.

And the second is when one puts the other outside the lists, either living or dead, whichever he should be. The body will be delivered by the judge to the Marshal for to grant pardon or do justice completely at our pleasure. And so if he is alive we wish and ordain that he ought to be raised up and disarmed by the King of Arms or heralds, his points cut, and all his harness thrown here and there around the lists, and then ought to be laid on the ground.

If he is dead, he shall likewise be disarmed, and there left to await our orders, which will be to pardon or do justice, just as seems good to us. But his pledges will be confiscated up to the satisfaction of the party, and the surplus of his goods confiscated to his Prince.

XVII. How the victor departs from the lists honorably.

Likewise we wish and ordain that the victor honorably should leave the field on horseback in the manner in which he has come in if he does not have excuse of his body, carrying the weapon with which he has defeated his adversary in his right hand. And the pledges and hostages will be delivered to him. And that concerning this quarrel he will not be required to answer any information to the contrary, nor any judge be able to compel him if he does not wish it. Because it transfers into a judicial matter, and judicial authority ought to be inviolately observed.

Likewise we wish and ordain that the horse as it is, and the arms of the defeated and all other things which came on his person or were brought for him belong by right to the Constable, the Marshals, or Marshal of the field, who therefore will have the keeping of them. Thus end the ceremonies, ordinances and statutes of France which belong to and are required for all pledges of battle made by conflict.

Now let us pray to God that He guard the right to the one who has it, and protect each good Christian from falling into such peril; for among all the perils which are, is that which one ought to fear and doubt, of which many a noble is found deceived having good right or not, too much relying on their tricks and their strength or by their presumptuous wrath. And sometimes, for the shame of the world, they deny or refuse peace or suitable judgments of which many times have then borne new penitences from old sins, and indifferent to the judgment of God. But he who complains and does not find justice, ought to seek God; and if it damages him, and without vainglory or ill will, for his good right alone, requires battle, he should fear neither trickery nor force, for the true judge will be for him.

If we compare this French ordinance to the Duke of Gloucester's rules for trial by battle issued in England ninety years later, we see a legal procedure that is also associated with royal authority and takes place in a high-status context. The Duke of Gloucester's rules could serve as a set of instructions to the Marshal and Constable of England, whose duty it is to supervise and arrange the duel. Despite the fact that the English tradition of using approvers continued, which therefore made one kind of duel routine, Gloucester's rules described a legal procedure accessible to a restricted class of people and supervised by high officers of state. Written by Thomas, Duke of Gloucester, for Richard II in a time of looming civil war to regulate gages of battle, much of the content is peculiar to that sort of contest.

Gloucester Ordinance, England, 1397 – royal ordinance

The King shall find the field to fight in. The lists shall be made and devised by the Constable. And the lists shall be considered to be sixty paces in length and forty paces in breadth in good manner, and firm, stable, and hard, and evenly made without great stones, and the earth shall be flat. The lists shall be strongly barred round about with a gate in the east and another in the west, with good and strong barriers of seven foot of height or more. And know that there should be false lists outside the principal lists between which the men of the Constable and the Marshal and sergeants of arms should keep and defend if any would make any offense or affray against the cries made...and these men should be armed at all points.

On the day of the battle the King shall be in a seat or in a scaffold and a place shall be made for the Constable and Marshal at the foot of the stair of the said scaffold where they shall be.

The appellant shall come to the east gate of the lists in such manner as he will fight, with his arms and weapons assigned to him by the court, and there he shall abide till he be led in by the Constable and the Marshal. And the Constable shall ask him who comes armed to the gate of the lists and what his name is and what is his cause. The appellant shall answer: "I am such a man -- A. de K. -- the appellant, who has come this journey, etc., to do, etc."... Then he shall open the gates of the lists and make him enter ... and also his counsel with him; he shall go before the King and then to his tent, where he shall abide till the defendant comes.

In the same manner shall the defendant come, except that he shall enter at the west gate of the lists....

And then the Constable shall command the Marshal to cry at the four corners of the lists in manner as follows: "Oyez, Oyez, Oyez. We charge and command by the King's Constable and Marshal that no one of great value and of little estate, of whatever condition or nation he may be, shall be so hardy henceforward to come nigh the lists by four feet or to speak or to cry or to make a face or token or semblance or noise by which either of these two parties A. de K., appellor, and C. de B., defender, may take advantage of the other, upon peril of losing life and limb and their goods at the King's will."

And afterward the Constable and the Marshal shall empty all manner of people from the lists except their lieutenants and two knights for the Constable and Marshal who shall be armed upon their bodies, but they shall have neither knife nor sword upon them nor any other weapon by which the appellant or the defendant may have advantage because of negligence in keeping them. But the two lieutenants shall have in their hands a spear without iron to separate them if the King wants them to leave off in their fighting, whether it be to rest them or any other thing whatsoever pleases him.

The Constable sitting in his place before the King as his vicar general, and the parties made ready to fight by the command of the King, the Constable shall say in a loud voice as follows: "Lessiez les aler"; (that is to say, "Let them go") and rest a while; "Lessiez les aler," and rest another while; "Lessiez les aler et fair leur devoir de par Dieu"; (that it is to say, "Let them go and do their duty in God's name.") And this said, each man shall depart from both parties, so that they may encounter and do that which seems best to them.

And if it happens that the King wishes to take the quarrel in his hands and make them agree without more fighting, then the Constable, taking the one party, and the Marshal, the other, shall lead them before the King, and when he has shown them his will, the said Constable and Marshal shall lead them to the one part of the lists with all their points and armor as they are found when the King took the quarrel in his hands as is said. And so they shall be led out of the gate of the lists together, so that the one shall not go before the other in anything; or by any way, for since he has taken the quarrel in his hands, it should be dishonest that either of the parties should have more dishonor than the other. For it has been said by many men of old that he that goes first out of the lists has the disworship...

Another ordinance or customary regulation survives from 14th-century Guyenne in the South of France. Like the previous two documents, it sets a standard for what is clearly a method of settling disputes accessible only to high-ranking people. In this case, because it is recording a set of civic privileges, the ordinance makes it clear that bourgeois or high-ranking citizens may be well qualified to use this procedure. Equipment, clothing, and arms permitted to the combatants are spelled out in detail. The scale of the substantial preparations seems comparable to those that might be needed for a long foreign expedition rather than a one-day conflict. Is this an attempt to keep participants from begging off because they have been unable to make preparations? The throwing of the gant (glove) as the pledge is noteworthy. Some of the technical terms for armor and weapons are defined in the glossary. A number of obscure terms for clothing and kitchenware are not. The non-military material has been included here only to indicate how well-equipped participants in a duel might be.

Guyenne Ordinance, SW France, 13th and 14th century – provincial ordinance

It is suitable that the speaker says, or tells his advocate the cause for which the combat will have taken place. The advocate, if he is wise, ought to solemnly declare that nothing which he says, either by ignorance, or by haste in speaking, to state article by article more or less, touching the material facts, neither harms, nor can be harmful to him or to his client, in all or in part; but he reserves to himself to add, diminish, correct and declare the next day, the day the deed commences, and the third also as above and the last day just as well as the first.

The one who makes the appeal ought to solemnly declare the same, …

Then the advocate ought to announce the facts affirmatively, with his companion standing by his side. During the whole time when he will speak, he ought to hold his hand on his head, or certainly hold him by the hand, and make him say all the words of the appeal, word for word.

Then he ought to affirm his appeal as follows showing the lord the man whom he wishes to appeal by [pointing with] a finger and hand, expressing himself thus:

"Lord, I say that this man who is there (and he indicates him) is false, a traitor, disloyal, a murderer; that he should not be in this court nor before any other he who in an ambush, on such a day, at such an hour, in such a place, with others, (which I reserve to myself to make known at a place and time) murdered and killed falsely, as a traitor, my brother, who he did not guard from him or from those who pierced him with a sword through the cote, from which blow he died. And this blow I have seen; and I have seen him take the bloody sword out of the body and the bloody hands and this, lord, I have seen, and I offer myself to prove it by sufficient men worthy of faith, if he dares to contradict it. And if, lord, you believe that some proofs by testimony ought not to be received, I, lord, put my body in proof that he is false and a traitor, just as I have declared; and I say, lord, that he will not dare to contradict it; and if he should do that I, lord, shall fight him in a closed field, with some arms which I reserve to declare and to choose; where I will make him say with his own mouth that he was a traitor, and in this matter I will leave him dead and vanquished on the field; and I deliver to you, lord, my gants, in pledge of battle. But I solemnly declare that if, perchance, on a given day I am not able, lord, to fulfill my intention, at the next day chosen and all the other days which you will assign to me, I will be there at that time and place."

And the adversary who is appealed, or his advocate ought to make the same solemn declarations, and ought to deny him, speaking in this way:

"Lord, I say that he lies falsely through his teeth."

And he ought to throw his gage. And if he is a bourgeois or other who ought to go to court right before the Mayor and the Jurats, and there ought to present him to the castle and there, the lord, in his sovereignty ought to assign a day for showing the arms which they have chosen, and the next day to discuss the choice of arms and the day of battle. Each champion ought to return at the hour of noon or before on his horse, with his harness and all which will be necessary for him, for, after this, the lord will allow nothing to be added to what he has presented there. On the day of the presentation of arms he who has made the appeal ought to present himself first, and the other afterwards; and if they intend to follow the customs and usage of France, they ought present first bodies and horses and then rest of that which pertains to the combat. One uses in common the same form in all partshorse.

And those who present themselves thus take care that on the day of combat that they ought to come to the field at the hour which the lord has assigned to them, dressed with all their arms for body and horse, for when they are on the chosen field, the lord will not allow them to retrace their steps, nor add anything to their equipment. The presentation can take place at any time of day, for it does not have a fixed time by custom, at least the lord does not assign it by his office. Said presentation having been done, the combatants present themselves with sureties, the next day, at noon, on the field, for the combat. When they are entering, if they are on horseback they are able to dismount with the permission of the lord; and when they are dismounted, it is the custom that they make the cross on the ground, which they kiss afterwards. And when they have stood up, they will go to their tent, where they should drink if they wish. Then, on one part and on the other, they should give to the lord their hostages who oblige themselves to submit their bodies to prison for two causes, namely that regarding some other provisions and some other duties they will make their agreements with the lord to follow the custom.

Likewise, if by some man of either party some damage occurs to the environs of the field they ought to repair it.

Then the lord has the combatants come to the middle of the field, and they swear two things by their hands: first, he who has appealed swears that he has appealed well and in full right, and that he has on himself to his knowledge no precious stone or amulet. Then the one who is appealed swears that the thing for which he is appealed is different and that he does not carry on himself to his knowledge any precious stones or amulets. The lord puts forward, either before or after, some sworn commissioners, charged to listen to the parties. The combatants then go to mount their horses and commence the combat.

The presentation of bodies the horses and the armors goes the same way at the moment of combat. One says to the lord: "My lord and judges, this man presents here his body against the other to do what he ought."

He then presents, to plead and support his person, his reasons and his right, his advocate, or his advocates except for what he could disavow if necessary.

On his body, he presents cloth breeches...

He presents underpants of cloth ...

trousers with belts and adorned fasteners ...

a pourpoint

chausses of linen and cloth,...

 iron shoes, with steel bands...

...adorned spurs

Leg armor in wood and iron

...banded steel cuisses...

headgear of hempen cloth and silk

... gorgets of cloth and iron, doubles and simples, decorated....

a bascinet, fitted with lames and mail, with braids and cords, of silk and hemp or of linen, with decorated camail, ...

harness and garnished *grinons* (?= head covering),

...a pourpoint equipped with steel bands...

... a coat of arms [an actual coat bearing heraldry?]

… a decorated belt, with the large dagger

… sharp swords with decorated belt

… adorned helmet, with the visor

… adorned maces

…an adorned shield

… swords and lances adorned with iron and other necessary fittings

… a horse, saddled

… braids, halters and reins adorned with leather and iron

… saddles with breastplates, girths and trimmed stirrup leathers.

… dyed coverings for the needs of his horse made of cloth, silks, linen and adorned with canvas,

… for the needs of his horse arms for the head, adorned.

… coverings of iron, with whatever suits him, in order to arm his horse …

…ensigns of cloth and silk

… linen, cords, kits (*or* cases), belts and this canvas, yarn and needles and points, an awl to make the needle pass, some sword belts for the use of his body and horse….

… diverse objects, for the needs of his body and to arm and shoe his horse.

… decorated serviettes, adorned dishes and plates, his bread, wine and water, his chickens, and almonds, fire and salt, pitchers, pots, his deep plates, hot plates, knives; some hay, some oats, some flour, some bran

… his doctor, some eggs, tow, linen, canvas, and some linen for ties and to sew up the wounds, and some extracts, brews, plasters and ligatures necessary to treat and cure his body and his horse,

And further it is good to know that the man has armed himself with jupons *de manges*(?) and *de fandas*(?) of a hammer, with gardebras of iron and leather, with avantbras of iron and leather, of one bascinet with camail and helm-cap, boots of iron and leather,

First, the appellant presents his body to the lord, and the ensemble of his armors, against the one being appealed, then he dismounts a little.

… also his chemises and culottes of linen and his high chausses adorned with kits and fastenings.

…his gaiters and shoes of leather, his chausses and his breeches of leather, his gorgerins of boiled leather, as well as his pitch-coated thread, his cords of thread and of silk and the other things necessary for such armors.

… the camail of boiled leather, with a pointed visor, adorned kits, just as it suits and he displays it; he presents then his adorned shield then his adorned leather shoes just as he ought to do.

He presents also his advocate to counsel him and to say his right and his reason; save that he solemnly declares to revoke it if there is need.

… his master armorer with his devices and his instruments, for the needs of his body and of his armors.

… physicians with the extracts, plasters, brews and ligatures necessary for his body.

…some wire, silk, cloth, cords, some pitch-coated thread, some kits, straps and a skin to make some kits, and any other thing that is needed.

…his needles for bast and others; scissors and razors, awls and bodkins, hammers and files.

… linen, tow, bands for the legs, wool, canvas, linen cloth grosse and fine, lard, liniments and olive oil.

… tables for eating, tablecloths, napkins, bread, wine, water, meat, salad, hens, fire, wood, salt, jugs, cups, pots, tripods, iron pans, dinner plates, salt cellars, knives, eggs, pepper, *agres* (?) of vinegar and a wax candle.

Treatise of the Points of Worship in Arms, England 1434 – treatise

Treatise of the points of worship in arms by Johan Hyll (Hill) Armorer Sergeant in the King's Armory 1434

Here follows for my lawful lords a treatise compiled by John Hyll, Armorer-Sergeant in the office of Armory under Kings Henry IV and V, concerning the points of worship in arms and how [a man] shall be diversely armed and governed by the support of favor of all the needs to cover increase and decrease where it is needed by the high command of the princes who have the power to ordain and establish it.

The foremost honor in arms is for a gentleman to fight in his sovereign lord's quarrel in a combat about treason, sworn within the lists, before his sovereign lord; whether he be appellant or defendant, he who wins the field has the honor. As for the appellant, either all armed by his own knowledge or by the counsel assigned to him before the Constable and Marshal, the counsel is ordained and bound to teach him all manner of fighting and subtleties of arms which belong to a sworn combat.

First he needs to have a pair of hose of corde without vampeys, the hose cut at the knees and lined with linen cloth cut on the bias as the hose is; a pair of red leather shoes thin laced and fretted underneath with whipcord and pursed; And above within lined with linen cloth three fingers in breadth double and bias from the toe and inkle above the wrist. And so behind at the heel from the sole half a quarter of a yard up this is to fasten well to his sabatons. And the same sabatons should be fastened under the sole the foot in two places, he needs also a petticoat of an overbody of a doublet, his petticoat being sleeveless, his *syses* three quarters about without a collar, and that other part no further than the waist with straight sleeves and collar and curtain eyelets in the sleeves for the avantbras and the rerebras.

Armed in this wise first behoveth sabatons, greaves and close cuisses with voiders of plate or of mail and a close breche of mail with five buckles of steel the fabric of fine leather. And all the arming points after they have been knit and fastened on him and he is armed, his points should be cut off.

And then a pair of close gussets strong slav cloth and that the gussets should be three fingers within his plates at both assises. And then a pair of plates at twenty-two pounds weight, his breast and his plates fitted out with wire or points.

A pair of rerebras fastened within the front plates with two forelocks before and three forelocks behind. A pair of avantbras close with voiders of mail and fretted. A pair of gloves of advantage which may be devised. A bascinet of advantage for the lists which is not good for any other combat but man for man save that necessity has no law, the bascinet locked, beaver and visor locked or hinged also to the breast and behind with two forelocks.

And this gentleman appellant when he is thus armed and ready to come to the field puts on a coat of arms of single tartan for better advantage in fighting. And his leg harness should be covered all with red tarityn which are called jackets. The covering of his leg harness is done so that the adversary shall not easily see his blood. And therefore also when his red hose for in all other colors blood will easily be seen, for in the old time in such a combat nothing should have been seen here save his bascinet and his gloves. And then tie on him a pair of saddlebags. Also it is fitting that the aforesaid counsel should go to the King before the battle and ask for lodging near the lists. Also the aforesaid counsel must arrange masses for him: the first mass of the Trinity, the second of the Holy

Ghost and the third of Our Lady or else the masses of any other
saint or saints for whom he has devotion.

And he should be watched all that night, having light in his
chamber all that night so that his counsel may know how he sleeps,
and in the morning when he goes to his masses his harness should
be laid at the north end of the altar and covered with a cloth that
the gospel may be read over it and at the last mass may be blessed
with the priest. And when he has heard his masses then he should
go to his dinner. And so is his arming in the form aforesaid.

And when he is armed and all ready then he should come to
the field in form before rehearsed, that his counsel are bound to
counsel him and to teach him how he shall govern himself in his
requests to the King or he when comes into the field and his entry
into the field and his governance in the field; for the said counsel
has charge of him before the Constable and Marshal until "Laissez
les aller" shall be cried. The which requests are thus that the said
appellant sends one by his counsel to the King to request from
him that when he comes to the barriers to have free entry with his
counsel, confessor and armorers with all manner of instruments
with bread and wine, himself bringing in an instrument that is to
say a chest or a pair of water bottles.

Also fire, coal and bellows and his chair may be brought into the
field by certain of his servants and set up there on the hour of his
coming that it may cover him and his counsel when he is coming
into the field, this aforesaid gentleman appellant coming to the lists
whether he will be on horseback or on foot with his counsel, confessor and other servants aforesaid having borne before him by his
counsel a spear, a long sword, a short sword and a dagger fastened
upon himself his swords fretted and this *waged* before the hilts
having no manner of points for and there be found that day on him
no points of weapons then fair, it shall turn him to great reproof.

And this gentleman appellant that comes to the barriers at the Southeast *sone*, his visor down. And he shall ask entry where the Constable and Marshal shall meet him and ask him "Who are you?" And he shall say "I am such a man" and tell his name to make good this day by the grace of God what I have said of such a man and tell his name before my sovereign lord and they shall bid him put up his visor and when he has put up his visor they shall open the barriers and let him in, men and his counsel before him and he shall go with his armorers and his servants straight to his chair with his bread, his wine and all the instruments that will belong to him save his weapons. And when he enters into the field that he bless him soberly and so twice where he comes to before his sovereign lord. And his counsellors shall do their obeisance before their sovereign lord twice before they come to the steps of his scaffold and he to obey him with his head both times.

Then when they shall meet and kneel down before their sovereign lord and he also they shall arise, or he arise, he shall obey him at his heed to his sovereign lord and then arise and when he is up on his feet he shall bless him and turn him to his chair and at the entering of his chair soberly turn his visage to his sovereign lord's wards and bless him and then turn him again and so go to his chair and there he may sit down and take off his gloves and his bascinet and so refresh him until the hour when his adversary approaches with bread and wine or with any other thing that he has brought in with him. And when the defendant his adversary comes into the field that he be ready armed again or that he come into the field standing without his chair to heed of his adversaries coming in and of his countenance may take up comfort of.

And when the defendant his adversary has come into the field and is in his chair then shall the King send for his weapons and he and the Constable and the Marshal examine them and if they be lawful they shall be kept in the field and cut the same day by the commandment of the King and the Constable and Marshal on the King's behalf. And then it is fitting for the aforesaid counsel to arm him and to make him ready against being called to his first oath and when he is called to his first oath that it is fitting to all his counsel to go with him to his first oath to hear what the Constable and Marshal say to him and what countenance he makes in his swearing. And when he has sworn they shall rise up by the commandment of the Constable and the Marshal.

And when he is on his feet he shall obey his sovereign lord and bless him and then return to his chair, his visage turned to his sovereign lord and in his going bless him twice by the way that he comes to his chair. And when he enters his chair he should soberly turn his visage to his sovereign lord wards and bless him and so go into his chair. Then it is fitting for his foresaid counsel to await where the defendant shall come to his first oath and that they shall be there as soon as he, to hear how he swears for he must needs swear that all that ever the appellant has sworn is false substance and all, and if he will not swear that every word and every syllable of every word substance and all is false and the counsel of the said appellant may right to wisely ask judgment by civil law of civil and reason of arms or after the judge is set there should be no plea be made before him that day.

And if so it is that the defendant swear duly then the counsel of the aforesaid appellant shall go to his chair again and abide there until they be sent for. And then shall they bring him to his second oath and hear how he swears and when he has sworn they shall go with him to his chair again in the form aforesaid. And when he is in his chair the said counsel shall await when the defendant comes to his second oath and hear how he swears and if he swears under any subtle term crooked or cavailing aforesaid counsel of the appellant may require the judgment. And if he swears in a proper manner then shall the counsel of the aforesaid appellant go to his chair again and abide there until they be sent for.

And then shall they bring him to his third oath and assurance. And when they be sworn and assured the said appellant with his counsel shall go again to his chair in the form aforesaid and there make him ready and fasten upon him his weapons and so refresh himself until the Constable and Marshal bid him to come to the field. Then shall his armorers and his servants clear the lists of his chair and all his instruments at the command of the Constable and Marshal. And it is fitting to the counsel of the said appellant to ask a place of the King before him within the bars upon his right hand that the said counsel of the appellant may come and stand there when they be discharged of the said appellant.

The cause is this that such pity may be given to the King if God wills that no one of them shall die that day for he may by his royal power in such a case take into his hand the aforesaid counsel of the appellant to abide in the said place until the King has given his judgment upon him – and then the Constable and Marshal shall deliver the aforesaid appellant by the command of the King to his aforesaid counsel to govern him of his going out of the field as well as they did of his coming in his worship to be saved in all that lies in him. And so to bring him to his lodging again to unarm him comfort him and counsel him. And some of his counsel may go to the King and common with him and know from the King how he shall be demeaned. This enarming here aforesaid is best for a combat of arrest with a sword, a dagger, an ax and a pavise til he come to the assembly, his sabatons and his jacket taken off. And then the author Johan Hill died at London in November in the thirteenth year of King Henry VI so that he accomplished no more of the compiling of this treatise God have mercy on his soul for his endless passion Amen.

Depiction of a judicial combat in an early 14th-century German law book, Sachsenspiegel, *illustrating the provision that the two combatants must "share the sun", i.e. align themselves perpendicular to the Sun so that neither has an advantage.*

Source: *Dresden Codex,* early to mid-14th century

Mithridates VI, king of Pontus, kills his nephew Ariarath VII with his sword; a deed from antiquity presented to the contemporary audience as a judicial duel. From a French translation of Giovanni Boccacio, presented to the Duke of Berry by Laurent de Premierfait in 1409.

Source: *Geneva,* Library of Geneva, Ms. fr. 190/2, 43r

By the late Middle Ages, the old Germanic foot duel with sword and shield had evolved into elaborate, specialized equipment, such as the spiked dueling shields seen here for a fight between commoners, and the sword with a heavy, spiked pommel carried by the fully armoured knights.

Source (top to bottom): *Rutland Psalter*, 62v; Codex Wallerstein, Cod.I.6.4°.2 96r, 105v.

A king watching a judicial combat. Documents relating to the office of marshal of England. Last quarter of the 14th century.

Source: *Cotton Nero* D. VI f.82.

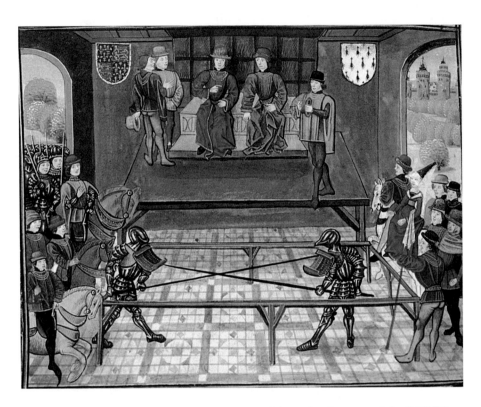

The Earl of Buckingham (Thomas of Woodstock) and the Duke of Brittany (John IV/V "The Conqueror", d.1399) fight with spears on foot at Vannes. High profiles feats of arms often blurred the line between martial sport and duel, though lacking in the legal justification for lethal combat.

Source: *Chroniques de Jean Froissart*, British Library, Royal 18 E I f. 139.

Detail of a miniature of the judicial combat of Jacques le Gris and Jean de Carrouges, showing the duel's gruesome conclusion.

Source: *Recueil des croniques d'Engleterre* BL Royal 14 E IV, f. 267v, c. 1483.

A 16th-century depiction of the mounted duel of Theobald Giss v. Seitz von Althaim, Bavaria, 1370.

Source: Paulus Hector Mair, *De Arte Athletica II*, Bayrische Staatsbibliothek Cod. icon. 393, 191v – 192r

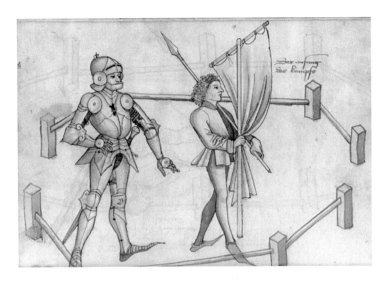

The Judicial Duel: Ceremony of the Day of Judgment. (Top) Each combatant enters the list to state their claim, dressed in their full battle-gear, as previously agreed upon by the parties. (Bottom) The two parties are seated at opposite ends of the list, while the agreed terms of the combat, from the smallest details of equipment, to how the combats will be resolved, are read. Note the coffins covered by crosses at their sides.

Source: Hans Talhoffer, *Fechtbuch*, MS Thott.290.2°

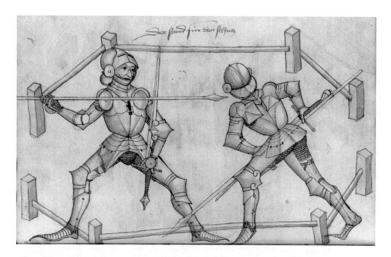

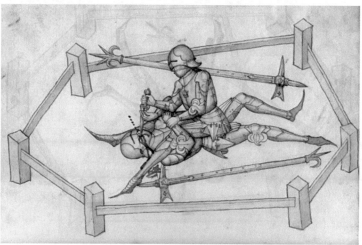

The Judicial Duel: Combat and its Bloody Resolution. The style and form of combat in the judicial duel was regulated by custom, often descending from ancient Germanic law, and might be fought on horseback, foot, or both. (Above) One form of German duel, illustrated at length by the 15th-century fencing master, Hans Talhoffer, was fought on foot and began with the casting of spears, followed by combat with two-handed swords. (Below) Although not mandated in all cases, the duel could very well end in death, and was expected to do in cases involving "high crimes" such as treason, rape, incest or heresy.

Source: Hans Talhoffer, *Fechtbuch*, MS Thott.290.2°

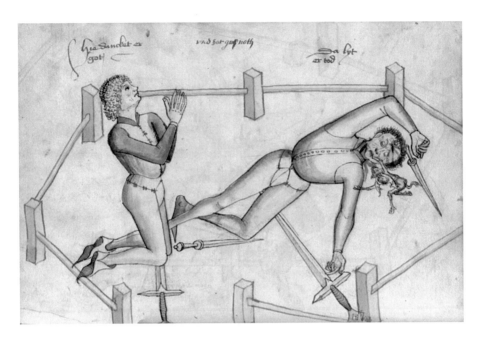

The Judicial Duel: The Judgment of God. Talhoffer ends his depiction of the duel with a reminder of its spiritual, as well as temporal, seriousness. The victor prays, both in thanks and for absolution of the murder he has committed, while the loser, having called on God to bear false-witness, has his soul dragged to hell by an imp. Whatever the folk-religious belief in the duel's spiritual authority, trial by combat had never been accepted by the Church, and ecclesiastical authorities spent centuries decrying its legal or spiritual legitimacy.

Source: Hans Talhoffer, *Fechtbuch*, Ms.Thott.290.2°, 137v

The Death of le Gris. Another depiction of the Carrouges-le Gris, duel, interesting here for its similarity to the resolution of the duel depicted in the fencing treatise of Hans Talhoffer, shown previously.

Source: British Library, Royal Ms. 14E.IV f-267v

Judicial duel between Marshal Wilhelm von Dornsberg and Theodor Haschenacker in the Augsburg wine market (1409). Dornsberg's sword broke early in the duel, but he succeeded to kill Haschenacker with his own sword. Their shields were kept in St. Leonard's Church outside Augsburg until they were destroyed in 1542.

Source: Paulus Hector Mair, De Arte Athletica II, Bayrische Staatsbibliothek Cod. icon. 393, 194r – 195v

A depiction of the lethal duel between Otto von Grandson and Gerhart von Steffis at Bourgen-Bress in 1397. Otto fell to his kness and Gerhart slew him with a lethal thrust of the axe's top spike into the back of his neck. From the Spiezer Chronik by chronicler Diebold Schilling (1483). Although created in the late 15th century, the the combatants are rendered in an interesting amalgam of late 14th and mid-15th century armour components.

Source: Bern, *Burgerbibliothek*, Mss.h.h.I.16

4.

A fight to the finish in Southern Germany, 1370

One of the most interesting and detailed 14th-century accounts of a judicial combat is recorded in a German manuscript compiled by Paul Hector Mair in the middle of the 16th century and preserved in Augsburg today. Both the script and the illustrations are spectacularly beautiful (and can be seen online – see bibliography). The manuscript was part of Mair's effort to preserve older traditions of the fighting art, and so the story of the duel between Theobald Giss and Seitz von Althaim may well follow a contemporary account. Giss and von Althaim represented competing noble factions in Bavaria and Swabia. The region was quite disorderly and cattle were stolen at an alarming rate. In 1370, Theobald Giss accused von Althaim of leading the rustling expeditions, and von Althaim turned the charge against him. This account is remarkable for the detail it preserves concerning the political background of the case, the legal procedures that preceded the actual duel, (not all of which are reproduced here) and the fight itself. The duel was longer than most others recorded and featured a long fight on horseback in which neither rival was injured, and then a heated foot combat during which Giss and von Althaim lost and then recovered their weapons. Von Althaim was victorious and he was extravagantly praised by his partisans and gained great honor for himself and no doubt for his noble faction.

Theobald Giss v. Seitz von Althaim, *De arte athletica* II, Bavaria , 1370 (16th century) – swordsmanship treatise

In the year 1369 no small controversy arose between the princes and nobles of Bavaria on both sides on account of the lands of Bavaria and Swabia. Then in this turmoil a certain noble, Theobald Giss, found the opportunity to slander Seitz ab Althaim, likewise a noble, charging him with having despoiled Bavaria, and driving out of Mechingen a numerous herd of cattle, cattle for plowing and many other animals and transferring all of them to Eppissburg. Moreover the people of Eppissburg received the said Althaimer as a guest and he fixed his domicile in that place … When therefore Althaimer found out about the letters deceitfully written to the duke by Theobald Giss … he sent letters to the petitioner Theobald, rebuking and imputing that he had written with a false mind to the Duke of Bavaria; he certainly affirmed that Eppissburg had never received him with hospitality and never on any occasion had he offered to invade Bavaria. Then also he had been granted the power to attack Bavaria in that place and supported by public letters sanctioned by the Duke's seal, by that matter never at any time should he be cheated of his reputation. Rather, it was Theobald Giss himself who was a robber and an informer.

Therefore a day was given to both, January 19 after the day of Saint Sebastian, in the year 1370, on which day joined with other nobles and guards and appeared in the public peace…

When the judges had heard the mutual accusations on both parts and all of them had consulted among themselves concerning the matter, both (combatants) were addressed as to whether the dispute could be peacefully settled by both the counts that were present, which if they agreed that they should report to him as soon as possible and return agreements by the will of both.

Both therefore were separately accused so that the business and controversy should be resolved, but neither side was willing to agree to these admonitions, but persevering with a strong and constant spirit, they both answered to the court, which without delay decreed that they should have their courage ready for performing single combat nor admitting any pacification, but rather to take care that justice, which they should be undertaking , should shine forth out of the combat.

And so when the judges recognized the unchangeable will in them both, they unanimously ordered that hostages be given and oaths made to almighty God, because they wished to fight according to royal law, statute and legislation also ordained by the judges. And they should without any delay stand by with a ready mind. As can be seen in the following picture.

Form of the oath by which they ought to guarantee to fight.

I [name] swear and give faith, to God the best and greatest and to the men of the region that I thither according to custom of royal law must be observed , and single combat which wholly the chief judges in like manner with additional judges will arrange according to royal custom, from the beginning of the fight to the end it must be fought in good faith, which I will perform, with God and all the saints helping me.

And so the oath having been taken by both for the guarantee of the fighters, the chief judge with the approval of the delegated judges declared the arms to be judged and agreed for both of them. To wit, in their combat, they were mounted on horseback without mail, and put on a linen tunic without sleeves with a wooden shield attached to the chest, made of wood and leather. Both were using spear, sword, dagger, fighting bareheaded, using only one gauntlet fitting the thumb. They fought on the day closest to the feast of Saint Agatha, which was Tuesday in February 1370, which happened to be acceptable to both, so they both prepared for the fighting. In the meantime in the Munich marketplace enclosures were prepared, sand was scattered, and other things were done very diligently for the future use of fighting.

When therefore the stated time for the fighting approached, both gathered at Munich with many nobles on either side brought along to assist them. At the same time the eminent entered the city for the fighting with accustomed pomp in accordance with the public peace, to whom equal honor was announced by Stephan prince of Bavaria.

Still on that day, in which they were to fight to the death, both were called by the chief judge that they should appear before the court wearing the arms conceded to them, and with the sword and spear indeed having been removed it was done without any delay.

When therefore they had appeared the judge had diligently scrutinized the arms of each and interrogated them about whether they were in good condition, and whether each within the said day was wounded nowhere on his body, and also whether they had rested after having made the journey, they allowed, responding to that questioning, that they were altogether fit.

Then the chief judge asked the judges accompanying and delegated to him whether the oath should be propounded according to the rite, law and custom of combat, or not. It was unanimously decreed by the judges, that these should be put forward according to royal custom and that they wished to contend in combat, commanding according to the custom of combat and the usual rite and practice, then the only fighters were called to the court, one of whom was to the left side of the chief judge, the other to the right on bended knee as the judge extended both hands and laid two fingers on the right hand giving an oath just as it was read aloud by the judge's scribe.

Form of an oath

You each give an oath according to royal custom and the custom of dueling to almighty God attesting that the very accusation which Althaim asserted against Theobald Giss by the law of the country should be true and he is moved to accuse not by hatred, envy or a malicious spirit. On the contrary, that Theobald Giss refutes the accusation by Althaimer and in that matter should be innocent. Therefore if one or both should be guilty, he should go to be severely punished by Almighty God, however he who has just cause if he should descend into the arena to fight, when they contend God will add to the matter through truth and by all the saints. After that they have sworn and their oath should be approved by the judges and legitimately done, both should withdraw into their lodging.

Meanwhile the supreme judge together with his delegated judges had prepared the place for the duel and examined whether according to the usual manner and rite either side should have arranged without fraud the enclosures and other things necessary for this purpose. When therefore they knew all rites to be done, the chief judge should plan to eat the preparatory meal.

When therefore he should have eaten, the judge around the first hour sent his messenger with two of his panel of judges to Althaimer, who was in his guest chamber, ordering according to the rite and custom of dueling that things should proceed by the aforesaid custom conceded by the court, that a horse should be sent to the dueling field and there he should expect the adversary he was going to fight. There Althaimer made no delays and putting on the habit used to fight, mounted up, and without delay sought the fighting enclosure. A large number of nobles likewise followed on horseback, and a certain noble from Gumpenberg presented a

spear to Althaimer. And so Althaimer came to the place chosen for
dueling and was received humanely by the judge, after the judge
had imposed the mandate, and turned his face within the enclosure toward the east, so that he waited there until he summoned
his adversary. Then at that point in time, the legate or messenger
having been sent, adding two others out of the court, he called
Theobald Giss who was in the other lodging waiting to come to the
fighting ground announcing that Althaimer was already present
in the enclosure.

Otherwise Giss had already reconnoitered from Althaimer to
the enclosure that he had been called to, he had armed first being
summoned by the chief judge, he was readily able to detect that
indeed he had not escaped the man, for the attire was granted by
judges, which many nobles followed for the same reason, and they
followed to the duel, for which a certain member of the family of
Bappenheim bore a spear to the designated place.

When therefore Theobald Giss went to the enclosure, the chief
judge from the region of Althaimer summoned him after both ar-
biters of Gumpenberg and Marscalchium from Bappenheim to be
called to his presence, and addressed them for this reason, enjoining
both sides that they should maintain justice in this struggle, unless they wish to harm their own renown, and be punished by
capital punishment, but rather that they'll decide according to his
own mandate and royal law that both, having given their faith, had
promised to do. Then immediately the arms of both were carefully
scrutinized, to see whether they had been matched fraudulently
contrary to the custom followed by the judges, both finding them
free from all deceit.

Then, after they had been found to be equally armed, the judge
announced by the herald or the trumpeter to the nobility, and the
common people, all and singular, that no one should immodestly

stir up conflict among the spectators, either by joking or in all seriousness, and they should avoid clamor and other disturbances,
but all should rather try for tranquility, adding that if any therefore
transgressed this, then he should be punished capitally.

Many nobles and commoners gathered from many places and
stood around the enclosure stand, among them there being some
princes who came there for the sake of watching the fight.

So when a cup of St. John was presented to the fighters, which
we call a final drink, the chief judge sat with the invited delegates
in a place erected by the enclosure. Arbitrators, indeed, posted
themselves on horseback anywhere in the enclosure next to the one
who bore a spear, and when the signal was given by the chief judge
to start the fight they forcefully rushed together, as shown in the
figure below. [See two-page illustration in the gallery.]

In the first clash they struck their shields forcefully with their
spears, with neither falling. Quickly they threw away the spears,
and having drawn their swords, they fought manfully behind their
shields and meanwhile neither of them were exposed. On account of
which both were judged brave men by all the spectators, so when for
half an hour they had fought with swords on horseback, and neither
had been wounded by the other, in a violent clash, in which Theobald was somewhat wounded, both were deprived of their swords
from the grave conflict, and had no other arms larger than daggers.
Then Giss as quickly as he could drew a dagger, while Althaimer
dismounted and seized a sword thinking to defend and protect
himself. On seeing this Theobald with a quick pace strove for a
superior position, and when he arrived, likewise he dismounted
and took a spear, which he saw while he was still mounted, only
with the other hand since Althaimer persisted too quickly in his
footsteps, and also seized the spear. So that Giss having neither
sword nor dagger seized the spear with both hands and attempted

to wrench it by force out of Althaimer's hand. When Althaimer saw Theobald throw his shield on his back and defend himself with no arms besides the spear, Althaimer threatened Theobald and proceeding quickly, directed a thrust at the enemy. Theobald Giss saw this, drew out his shield which hung from his back trying to catch the sword tip, but Althaim more energetically thrust that sword, near to the navel, sticking it into the body of the adversary below the shield. Theobald was alarmed by that wound, and bent his body desiring to seize the spear, but Althaimer thrust his sword again near the groin as far as the hilt. Even having received such a severe wound Theobald refused to surrender, therefore Althaimer rose up and inflicted a large wound on his head. Then for the first time Theobald turned to God, and commended himself to divine grace. Then both umpires quickly approached and comforted him, supporting his head on his shield; but at that very moment he expired.

After Giss had died, Althaimer, unharmed and completely uninjured in his body, approached the judges and asked whether he had strongly rebuffed the injury inflicted on the King by Giss, and fighting honestly and legitimately had obtained rightful victory. The judges responded that he according to royal law had by right defended his renown, and legitimately by fighting preserved it, and they affirmed that he had honestly gained the victory.

Afterwards Althaimer gave great thanks to almighty God with hands lifted up to heaven then brought back to the enclosure, [according to the laws?], Althaimer was accepted most graciously and with great applause by his companions who favored his faction. In contrast those who favored the party of Theobald Giss lamented and mourned and committed him to the tomb with great sighs and sadness to grieve. All however on account of this duel lifted Althaim with praises up to the stars! From this affair he won great authority for himself and brought forth immortal praise.

5.◆

Two famous 14th-century duels: Glarains v. Lignaige, Carrouges v. Le Gris

The 14th century seems to have produced a standardized form of duel that could be used for the three capital crimes: murder, rape and treason, and in some cases, other crimes as well. In 1375, the bastard of Glarains, a Frenchman taking part in a siege of an English-held castle provoked Perrot Lignais, a Gascon serving the English, into agreeing to a duel. Perrot had offended Glarains by making accusations against the French lord of Montravel, who had supposedly defaulted on ransom payments to Perrot Lignais. Perrot made such broad and inflammatory accusations against Montravel (who was not present at the siege) that Glarains felt that his and his companions' honor as fighting men was being called into question. This seemingly trivial incident caught the attention of many of those present, in particular, that of the Duke of Bourbon, commander of the French army in which Glarains served. Bourbon lent his authority – which as a captain on campaign was equivalent to that of a king—to the proposed duel.

He provided list barriers, tents and chairs for the combatants and their friends. He also set a limit to the fight; when Glarains seemed on the verge of killing Perrot, Bourbon halted the combat. This reluctance to allow a duel to continue to the bitter end is a feature of non-judicial deeds of arms of this era. Was this in fact a duel? Elements from judicial and non-judicial deeds are both present. Our unique source for the event calls it a *gaige*, but what crime was committed is uncertain. It is not murder, rape, or treason.

Glarains v. Lignaige, France, 1375 (1429). *The Chronicle of the Good Duke Louis of Bourbon* – biography

XXXIV. While the Duke of Bourbon was present in his army the bastard of Glarains fought for the quarrel of the lord of Montravel, a Gascon Englishman.

While the Duke of Bourbon considered and imagined how one could take the place, it happened that one Vespers, in the night watch, an English Gascon and one of the men of the Duke of Bourbon had words together; that Gascon was Perrot de Lignaige, and the man of Bourbon was called the bastard of Glarains. For Lignaige had said that the lord of Montravel, who was his prisoner, had broken his faith to him. And if he wanted to say the contrary, he should come forward, and he would fight him, or if yet none there who wish to maintain him, likewise he would fight him. To this the bastard of Glarains responded, "I am neither friend or relative of the lord of Montravel but if you have as great a talent for fighting as you appear to, tomorrow I will fight you before M. the Duke of Bourbon in such a quarrel so that if I defeat you, you will be my prisoner, and if you do I will be yours; and this you ought not at all refuse, if you have the desire to fight, for this is the life of arms." Concerning this the Englishman said that he would speak to M.

Robert Chennel, his captain, and that he would make his response. And the bastard of Glarains answered that he held securely to his most redoubtable lord, the Duke of Bourbon, who was very agreeable to him, for the Duke refused nothing to him which touched the bastard's honor. And so, for this time, the two separated. And this Perrot de Lignaige was to make a response to the bastard of Glarains, before noon or Vespers, which he did; and that he had permission from his captain to fight on the third day provided that the bastard of Glarains guaranteed it. He sent him surety and safe conduct from the Duke of Bourbon for him and 14 companions, and for which eventually the Duke of Bourbon had the lists made and the third day the Englishman Perrot de Lignaige came and the Duke of Bourbon receive him grandly and honorably and because the thing was before him, Lignaige found his beautiful tent pitched in the lists, for him to take off his armor, and to receive his companions who would come with him, and the bastard likewise, and each had his chair. And when they were in their chairs they were asked if they had anything more to say, and they said no. Immediately the heralds cried "do your duty!" So they joined battle and they made a fine fight, four blows on each other with their swords, after the throwing of lances, but the bastard of Glarains drove his adversary Perrot de Lignaige back a good six paces In the midst of it, the bastard threw himself the length of his sword, seized the Englishman Lignaige in his hands and, holding tight, bore him to the ground and throwing himself on him, lifted his visor, and gave him three blows with his gauntlet on the face, and then the Englishman who felt himself injured and ill-used surrendered shouting so loud that one could hear him well. But notwithstanding the bastard drew the sword of the Englishman and was ready to kill him with it when the Duke of Bourbon said it was enough and plenty had been accomplished. Whereupon he had them removed at that point: for he

in no way wished that the Englishman should die because the affair
had been done before him; and this good deed was turned to the
Duke of Bourbon's high honor.

In the next decade, a notorious judicial duel took place in Paris between Jean
de Carrouges and Jacques le Gris. We are fortunate to have a very detailed account
of the trial; indeed, we have accounts from different points of view. The cause
was an alleged rape of Marguerite, Carrouges' wife, by a squire named Jacques
le Gris. The two men knew each other well. Both were nobles from Normandy
and part of the household of the count of Alençon, which complicated the
issue, as did the fact that it was a classic "he said, she said" situation. Carrouges
got no satisfaction from his attempts to prosecute Le Gris through the usual
methods. Frustrated, Carrouges eventually petitioned the royal courts for a trial
by battle. We are fortunate to have much of the documentation generated by
this petition as legal experts in the *parlement* (high court) of Paris examined the
case. The *parlement* eventually approved the trial. Perhaps more importantly,
the young King Charles VI, a man who thought of himself as champion of
chivalry, became very interested and indicated his desire to be present for the
event, despite the fact that his government was in the throes of launching an
invasion of England. The King's enthusiasm reflected a popular excitement. A
huge number of people turned out to witness the combat. The spectacle was
all the more compelling because Lady Marguerite was also risking her life. If
her husband and champion lost, she would be considered to have made a false
accusation and would be burned.

The duel itself is one of the best described judicial combats that we have from
the late Middle Ages, though one could wish for more precision. Carrouges
was victorious, killing Le Gris and through his victory justifying his wife's
accusations – at least in theory. In fact, the duel and its result continued to be
controversial for a long time thereafter. One of Jacques le Gris' advisors, Jean
le Coq, wrote a legal memo describing his lawyerly doubts about the legitimacy
of the whole procedure. Later still, rumors circulated that Carrouges' wife had

been mistaken in her attacker and that once she realized this, she had retired to a nunnery from shame and a desire to seek forgiveness for her mistake. We are also told that Carrouges found it wise to leave France on pilgrimage, because he had used up the good will of a great many people in his single-minded prosecution of Jacques le Gris. Superficially, the duel had settled the question of guilt and proof, but in fact, it seems that the issue had divided the community. The "winners," although they made their point and survived grave danger, found themselves treated as pariahs.

Carrouges v. Le Gris, the legal battle, Paris, 1386. *Chronique du Religieux de Saint-Denys* – chronicle account:

The duel of Lord Jean de Carrouges with Jacques le Gris

The single combat of Jean de Carrouges with Jacques le Gris, accused of the rape of Jean's wife, gives plain proof to posterity how blameworthy it is to follow rumor in uncertain matters, in the way that leafy branches are bent by every breeze, for the matter may escalate (lit. progress) from this to vengeance.

This wicked treason seemed all the worse because both men were of Norman origin, serving in the household of the Count of Alençon, and had been joined since youth with the closest bonds of friendship. Many, feeling pity for the lady who had lost her chastity, asserted that Jacques justly was defeated, but afterwards it was established that some other squire was the author of the crime.

This traitor, in the absence of the husband, impelled by the fires of evil desire, undertook this most abominable crime under the false name of friend. In the guise of a visitor he entered the home like a thief aiming at her chastity. After dinner had been concluded, the lady, unaware of his evil design, had led him about like a good friend here and there and taken him to the guest chamber. Then he was unable to conceal his savage intention. For immediately he began to confess his love, and to implore, and to mix gifts with prayers and to harass the woman's spirit in every way. And when he fearfully saw her constant spirit, improper love made him bold, and throwing her down with his left arm he robbed the storeroom of her chastity and gave the victory to desire. Nevertheless the woman so vilely treated did not accuse the author of the crime.

On the return of the husband, however, tears and sobs of mourning appeared. When he asked if she were all right, she replied, "No, of course not, for how can a woman be well when she has lost her chastity? There is the mark of another man in your bed, beloved husband of mine, and thus Jacques le Gris has turned from a faithful friend into an enemy. Yet although my soul is innocent, death will testify that my body has been so greatly violated, unless you give your right hand and word that the rapist will not go unpunished."

The evil crime shook up the man, who called together his relatives and reassured the troubled woman, removing the guilt from the one who had been forced to the author of the crime. He argued that it is the mind that sins, not the body, and where consent is absent, so is guilt. But he was unable to convince her.

Repeated complaints by day and night persuaded the husband to demand most vehemently justice against the guilty man. When he had presented himself before the King and his barons and had reported the enormity of the crime in order repeatedly and importunately, he finished by saying, "If this wicked traitor denies he used deceit and violence against my most beloved wife, I cannot refuse to engage him in single combat."

At length the King granted his assent, as long as the knight's demand was judged by his *parlement* to be a just one. Once the advocates for either side had made their arguments, it was decided that since the truth could not be known because of the problems with witnesses, so that human judgment could not ascertain the good faith of either side, the royal sentence should be put into execution, on the day of St. Thomas, the twenty-first of December.

Extract of the registers of the parlement of Paris in the presence of the King. Paris 1386 – legal documents

Between Lord Jean de Quarrouges, knight, appellant and challenger in a case of pledge of battle on one part, and Jacques le Gris, defender on the other part, and for the occasion of this that the said knight said and maintained against the said squire that he, with the aid of a man named Adam Louvel had forced his wife, and, the demands and defenses of the parties having been heard, it was ordered that the same parties provide their deeds and reasons in writing from the court in the manner of a memoir, and having seen them, the court appointed them as from the reason to pleading of the defense.

Likewise it is further ordained that the said parties and each of them should provide pledges and surety to appear or return there as many times as they are ordered by the King or the court.

And this having been done those who follow constitute pledges for the said knight to come to do it in person, and at the time that the King will order it.

The Count of St. Pol
The Count of Valentinois
The Lord of Torcy
The Viscount of Uzes
Lord Guichard Dauphin
The Seneschal d'Eu

and for the said squire they constituted pledges, and do likewise in person:

The Count d'Eu

The Lord of Foillet

The Sire de Torcy

The Sire de Coigny

The Sire d'Anviller

And Lord Philippe de Harecourt.

II.

Saturday, the 15th day of September 1386

Today in the court a halt has been announced in the said case, that is to say that the court had adjudged pledge of battle between the said parties, and with this ordained that the said parties provide new hostages and guarantees, notwithstanding those who were formerly given as is said above. And for this deed those who follow may constitute pledges and guarantees for the said knight, body for body and goods for goods, and each one for all to render and bring and make comparison the said knight all the days which to him are assigned by the King or his court there where it will be ordained:

The Viscount of d'Uzes

The Lord of Hengest

Lord Jacques de Montmor

Lord Gerard de Bourbon

Lord Philippe de Cervoles

Lord Gerart de Grantval

And Lord Philippe de Florigny

And the said knight, that is to say Lord Jean de Quarrouges, has promised to compensate the said pledges.

And for the said Jacques le Gris:

Regnault d'Angennes

Jehan Beloteau

Guilles d'Acqueville

Jehan de Fontenay

Gibert Maillart

Et Pierre Beloteau.

And the said Jacques le Gris has promised to compensate the said pledges and through the said guarantee the said Jacques le Gris is released completely, under the agreements customary with pledge of battle, up to the said next day of St. Martin next coming, and between the two nothing else is ordained by the King. He has chosen his domicile in the hotel of the count d'Alençon at Paris.

III.

Saturday 24th September 1386.

The King our lord has sent to the court concerning certain sealed letters saying it suits him that the day on which the battle ought to be done between Lord of Quarrouges and Jacques le Gris, which ought to be the 27th day of the month of November, should be moved back to the Saturday next after Christmas next to come, which days he ordered to be signified to the parties.

And for this, today the court in the person of the said Jacques and in the person of the said Quarrouges has signified the same postponement and outcome, had the said letters read in their presence. Notification having been given, the people of Quarrouges and Jacques le Gris are required by the court to be released just as they were before.

So the court having seen that the aforesaid letters, which said that the matter should be postponed at its current juncture (more literally, as is), ordered that the words of Quarrouges and Jacques le Gris are published under the customary agreements for pledge of battle, up to the said Saturday next after Christmas to come, including the renewal of the guarantee which they have given at another time.

This having been done they have constituted pledges for the said Quarrouges, body for body and wealth for wealth each for all those who follow:

Lord Regnault de Braquemont, knight

Lord Robin de Thibouville,

Lord Robert de Torcy,

Lord Merle de Virjus

Lord Gui de Saligny.

For the said Jacques le Gris

The Lord le Galois d'Arcy, chevalier

Mathieu de Varennes

Jehan de Montvert

And Jehan Beloteau

Carrouges v. Le Gris, the combat, Paris, 1386. *Chronique du Religieux de Saint-Denys* – chronicle account

It was decided that the coming combat would be located next to the walls of St. Martin-des-Champs. It was held in the presence of the King and the princes according to custom, and a huge crowd of common people assembled. Both men entered the lists ready for the uncertain trial of combat. And when the Marshal gave the signal for the attack, they dismounted, let their lances of war drop, and proceeding at a gentle pace, they dashed against each other courageously and with spirit. In this first rush the other man pierced Lord Jean's thigh with his sword; and this blow would have done him much good if he had held the lance in that wound. But when he immediately drew it out, it was covered in blood, and the sight, rather than stunning the wounded man, made him bolder.

Meanwhile, great horror paralyzed the spectators for a long time, and no one spoke or breathed, held as they were between hope and fear, until Jean gathered his strength, and advancing, shouted "This day will decide our quarrel." With his left hand he seized the top of his opponent's helmet, and drew Jacques toward him and then pulling back a little, threw Jacques to the ground where he lay weighed down by his armor. Jean then drew his sword and killed his enemy, though with great difficulty, because he was fully armored.

Although the victor many times asked the defeated man while he was lying there to confess to the truth, the vanquished completely denied the event; but after all he was condemned, according to the custom of the duel, to be hanged from a gibbet. Thus the mother of errors, the stepmother of good counsel, rash cruelty occasioned this unjust duel. Afterwards everyone found out who had committed the foul rape, when someone else confessed while being condemned to death. The aforesaid lady took note of this, and thinking over the fault in her mind, after the death of her husband became a recluse and took an oath of perpetual continence.

Jean le Coq, Note concerning the duel of Jacques le Gris, Paris, 1386 – legal memo

Item a note that on the Sabbath after the birth of Our Lord 1386, which day was the feast of Blessed Thomas after Christmas, there was a duel fought between Jacques le Gris and Lord Jean Carrouges, behind the walls of St. Martin in the Fields, and the said Jacques was overcome and killed; and I have a troubled conscience about whether it was God's vengeance, and thus was seen by many who saw the duel, because the said Jacques, against the advice of his counsellors, was unwilling to help himself by privilege of clergy, although he was a cleric unmarried and defendant; and this I know because I was a member of his counsel. Others however saw that it was God's vengeance, because all reported commonly that he was guilty of the crime because the duel was decreed: of whom many affirmed the contrary nevertheless by oath by the said Jacques, namely that he never had done it, nor was he guilty , which I leave to his conscience. Likewise, note that the Great Council made lists similar to those of Gisors, which had been made two hundred years before; but it was said that it ought not be compared to those, because they were made for two men who fought on foot and not on horseback. The lists however of St. Martin were enclosed in the manner of the lists of Gisors, because they were made earlier on account of a voluntary combat, which it was believed to have taken place between Lord Gui de la Trimolle, Lord of Salyaco, and a certain Englishman, Lord Peter de Courtenay. There follow presumptions against the said Jacques le Gris, which I have, and many others. Fourth, because after the pledge was adjudicated he was ill. Fifth, because not much before entering the field he had been made a knight. Sixth, because although he was **defensor militum**, fiercely he seized his adversary the footman, although he had had an advantage, if he had been made a knight. Seventh, because although Carrouges had been weakened by fevers which he had had for a long time and it was obvious or apparent that the said Jacques was strong, nevertheless the said Jacques was defeated, miraculously, because the said Carrouges was unable to help himself. Eighth, because the wife of Carrouges was constant, always saying that the deed had taken place, both in childbirth and on the day of the duel: to which duel she was taken on a cart, but quickly was taken back by the King's order. Ninth, for he spoke weakly about the previous agreement talking with the presiders about the agreement. Tenth, because once he asked me whether in word or deed I should doubt him, because he saw me thinking. Eleventh, because he said to me that when he had heard rumors that Carrouges wished to prosecute him on this cause he was quickly confessed by a priest. Here followed presumptions for him.

First, because he always affirmed through oath that he had never done it, and he prayed to God, that he should help him in his affair, insofar as he was in the right, and not otherwise and I saw this done by him twenty times and he did it the day of the duel. Second, because he petitioned all the religious of Paris that they should pray to God for him, that should wish to help him insofar as he was in the right, and according that he was innocent of that deed, and that he never had done it, and not otherwise; and thus he did on the day of the duel. Third, because he was a man of good status and respectability. Fourth, because no one is unmindful of their salvation, etc. Fifth, because the lord of Alençon wrote to the King and the lords his uncles, saying that the said Jacques was not guilty. Six, many knights affirmed that he was with the Lord Alençon the whole day continuously during which the adversary said he had done the deed, and many days continuously before. Seventh, because Adam Lovel who was said to be guilty of the same crime was tortured, as well as the maid who was said to have been in the house of Carrouges that day, and they had confessed nothing. But some said that he was unwilling to confess anything because had confessed over this deed and he was not bound to confess at any later time, because it would be an insult for his relatives and friends, and somehow he confessed against the action of Lord Alençon, who had asserted that Jacques was not guilty of that deed. Nevertheless the truth about this deed was never known.

6. ◆
Duels and high politics

In the warlike 14th century we see a tendency to interpret political conflicts as treasonous crimes, extraordinarily vile, which could and perhaps should be resolved by judicial combats. If the two combatants were on opposite sides of an ongoing war, a duel might seem even more appropriate, because the question of jurisdiction might otherwise be a doubtful one.

In 1353, Henry, Duke of Lancaster (Henry of Grosmont), one of Edward III's most important generals, accused Otto, Duke of Brunswick (in Lower Saxony in Germany) of plotting to seize Henry while the Englishman was going to Prussia to take part in a crusade, with the intent of turning him over to his enemy, Jean, King of France. Otto angrily rejected this accusation and challenged the Duke of Lancaster to face him in arms. Otto charged Henry with lying and said he would maintain [that Henry's accusations were lies] by his own body and strength, as it was the duty of good and loyal lords to do.

The duel however did not proceed in a straightforward manner. Curiously, Otto proposed that King Jean, the very person he supposedly had plotted with against Lancaster, should preside over the duel, and Lancaster agreed. Perhaps even more curiously, Jean, according to some accounts, used the excuse of the duel to open negotiations with both dukes with the intent of improving relations with England. When Henry and Otto met in Paris to fight they allowed Jean to issue a verdict in which the very appearance of the two dukes was seen as increasing both men's honor. Fighting, ruled the King, was therefore unnecessary. Whatever the cause of the initial accusation, the duel was transformed into a move in a large diplomatic dance. Once again we see that the fighting part of a duel could be a quite secondary part of the whole effort to resolve a dispute. Likewise, judicial duels were now a privilege associated with high-ranking warriors rather than routine law.

Lancaster v. Brunswick, France, 1353. Henry Knighton, *Chronicon* – chronicle account

When therefore the Duke of Lancaster had come to Cologne, it was reported to the Duke of Lancaster by a certain knight that the Duke of Brunswick had orders from the King of France that he should seize the Duke of Lancaster who was on pilgrimage against the enemies of Christ. He still held his journey by which he set out and securely was led through diverse companies, but before his coming to Prussia, a truce for many years was reached between Christians and pagans, which much displeased him. But he turned around and came to Cologne, and there he related in the presence of many magnates that Duke Otto of Brunswick had imagined he would capture him and prevent him from taking his holy pilgrimage, both him and his companions when he did not commit a crime as far as he knew, nor did he have any acquaintance with him. And he further said that it was not fitting for such a duke to seize wrongfully such a knight on a foreign pilgrimage, who had taken nothing evilly with him, and if he desired to have something to do with him he should find him prepared in those things which pertained to the order of knighthood. When this was recited in the presence of the Duke of Brunswick he immediately without delay deceptively sent a letter to England to the Duke of Lancaster, in this form:

Otto by the grace of God Duke of Brunswick, seigneur of Thuringia, son of the grand Duke of Brunswick, to the excellent prince and noble Duke of Lancaster. Know that the words which you said personally with your own mouth in the sovereign church of Cologne named St. Peter, the Friday next after Easter past, before the noble prince Markes of Juliers and many honest knights and squires in the presence of the citizens of the same city evilly, basely and dishonestly were lies and were by no means true. Which things we maintain against you by our body and our goods just as a good and loyal seigneur is held and obliged to show towards an evil and dishonest and bad man. This we will do between the castle of Guines and St. Omer, either there or where the King of France will indicate a certain place. For in this matter, you and your people it having been forsworn by the aforesaid lord, are forbidden defiance. Concerning this, pray that you return an answer, written under your seal, with the bearer of this message.

Given at Querougaron etc.

Henry, Duke of Lancaster, wrote back to him, that on a certain day assigned to this case, he would be ready and by the grace of God that which truth demanded to be defended by his own body. And he prepared himself and went to Calais with fifty knights and a multitude of vigorous warriors. And when he was approaching Guines, Lord Jean Clermont Marshal of France met him with a fine multitude of armed men, and received him with honor namely in the fortnight before Christmas, and had him led with great honor as far as Hesdin, where James, Lord of Bourbon, met him with a strong company and led him to Paris, and showed him as much as he could of honor and reverence and all of his people. And in his entry to Paris he met a great number of nobles and magnates, receiving him with honor. And so great a multitude of foreign

citizens and commoners appeared that never so many in these
days were seen in that city and all showed him the highest honor
in their way. And immediately, the King of France sent for him to
come to him in his palace, and received him with great honor. The
King of Navarre, relative of the duke was above all pleased to have
him near him, and more wisely did everything for him. Before the
day of the battle the nobles negotiated among the parties but they
made little progress towards peace.

The day of battle arrived and they entered the lists with the
King of France and the whole crowd looking on, and having been
devoted to the sacrament of the Lord they presented an oath as to
the truth of the matter with, as is the practice of fighting men. Then
they mounted the destriers just as men prepared to fight. And it
was said that you did not see a more elegant or ferocious knight
than the Duke of Brunswick stood out before the performed oath,
which having been done his face wasted away and turned pale.
From that there were many reviling his complaint was not true, or
too presumptuous. And he bore a horse with a sad and pale countenance, and it was said, he did not have the light-heartedness, nor
the power gracefully to grasp the sword, the shield, and a spear,
and all other things that pertained to him, but as it were stunned
and disturbed completely worn out he shivered and three times he
upset his shield while receiving it. Finally from the counsel of his
friends he gave up his quarrel and abandoned his cause altogether,
committing himself in things high and low according to the orders
of the King of France. The Duke of Lancaster always stood in his
place, with a cheerful and elegant face, anticipating the fight as
was fitting for a knight to fight for truth. And everyone marveled
about his firm bearing. And he entirely refused forego the combat;
and he said that before entering the lists he was able to be strongly
inclined toward peace through the discussion of the counsel of his

friends; but after they entered the fighting ground on horseback, and the rest prepared what such a business required, with the King and magnates and all the people gathered to decide the truth of the cause it should be dishonor and reproach for the Duke of Lancaster to withdraw from the place without doing the deed, to the mockery of the whole English nation. And he said, he was unwilling to leave the place by whatever treaty or peace agreement unless he should have combat nor in any way did he wish to renounce battle unless by saving his honor and his blood and the laws of his Lord the King of England and the whole realm of the English at least insofar as it is so that the English people through him should not incur the reproach of shame but his honor should be saved completely, nor he should anticipate any other grace which God should wish to confer on him.

Then Otto Duke of Brunswick, just like a man defeated, placed himself according to the disposition and orders of the King of France asserting that he did not wish to start a conflict nor occasion insult to the Duke of Lancaster and concede his claim without some condition of honor being reserved to himself, in the highest honor of the Duke of Lancaster and his people.

[The] consiliarii of the Duke of Lancaster. [eleven named, more unnamed ones referred to].

Then the King of France made high cheer and concord between the dukes. Afterwards the King of France led the Duke of Lancaster here and there showing him many delights which he proposed to confer on him, and the duke wished to have none of them except a single thorn from the crown of Jesus Christ, which the same duke left in his collegiate church which he founded under the castle of Leicester.

During the 14th century there are a number of cases where disputes about military matters overlapped with accusations of treason. One documented case from England (or more accurately, the English military establishment) took place in 1380. A squire named Thomas Katrington, who had been entrusted with the command of a fortress in Normandy, surrendered it to the French. The English, or some of them, believed that Katrington should have been able to hold onto the fortress, as he had (by their reckoning) sufficient men and supplies. The English owner of the castle, Sir John Annesley, was particularly incensed and eventually challenged Katrington to a trial by battle. There was controversy as to whether this was an allowable use of judicial combat – military men could visualize all too clearly that they might be the target of such an action themselves, if unhappy companions saw some advantage in second-guessing their judgment. Further, surrendering a strong point when the military situation of the defenders seemed hopeless was commonplace. After much debate it was decided that since the alleged crime had not taken place in England, trial by battle was an allowable remedy. The chronicler Thomas Walsingham gave a dramatic and detailed account of the actual fight, which ended with the collapse of Katrington from overheating and exhaustion. Katrington died soon after.

Two features of this case are worth noting. First, it was a case that grew out of war and involved men who were active warriors. It seems that many if not all English captains thought it logical that the dispute should be settled by combat. Second, the dispute was, right from the beginning, seen as a political conflict; important peers supported either man.

Annesley v. Katrington, England, 1380. Walsingham, *Historia Anglicana* – chronicle account:

At this time a novelty was seen in England, when more unusual things drew more people to watch the show, since human nature enjoys not only variety but the unusual. A certain knight, named John Annesely, in the parliament which was rightly called "the

Good Parliament" in the time of the Lord King Edward, the third after the Conquest, placed the mark of treason on a squire, Thomas Katrington, formerly keeper of the castle of the Holy Savior which Lord Chandos had built in France in the isle of Cotentin, because it is said that Katrington had sold the said castle to the French for an incalculable sum of money, when he lacked neither means of defense or victuals: in that cause he wished to fight that squire according to the law of arms. On account of his wife, to whom it should have been an inheritance, through proximate affinity the said John Chandos should have expected the lordship of the castle, if it had not been treacherously alienated by the said Thomas. The aforesaid Thomas for this reason was arrested and imprisoned accordingly, but soon after this, when the duke (John of Gaunt) was allowed anything he liked, while the King, his father was spending his last days, it was resolved upon (it was said) by Lord Latimer, whom the squire had served in peace and in war, in just things and unjust, in the truth and in untruth. Nor was John Annesley able by his outcry able to have an effect during that whole time, some asserting that it would be against the laws of the Kingdom, that someone of that same kingdom for any cause should fight by such a law [= the law of arms?] in the Kingdom. They who opposed the most were those who feared the mark of a similar punishment. But finally under pressure from the judges and the leading soldiers of the region, it was determined that for an external cause, as in the present case, which did not originate within the limits of the Kingdom, and for transmarine possessions, it was permissible for someone to fight a duel, if the Constable and Marshal of the realm have been notified about the case and in their presence the duel was accepted.

Therefore, the day of the battle was set and in the meantime the necessities for the duel were prepared in the court at Westminster, namely the boundaries which they call "lists," made of the strongest

wood, as though to last forever. And when the set day arrived, they
came from all parts of the Kingdom to the unaccustomed spectacle
of battle, and the number gathering in London exceeded, according
to the testimony of many, the great number of those who gathered a
few years before for the King's coronation. Also the same day, early
in the morning, the King with his nobles and the common people,
having entered the place as was the custom, the knight in armor,
astride a destrier becomingly ornamented. For the accuser ought
to enter first, and await the entry of the defendant. Then, after a
certain hour the squire was called to defend his cause, in this form
- "Thomas Katrington, defendant, you are to prepare to defend thy
cause, for which Lord John de Annesley, knight and appellant, has
appealed to you in public and in writing." But this was done three
times by the voice of the herald of war. The third announcement
being complete the squire appeared armored and riding on a destrier bearing a horse-covering splendidly and displaying the arms
of the said Thomas. As soon as he came to the lists he dismounted
so that the Constable should not claim it, if he should enter the lists.
But his astuteness gained him nothing: for the horse, running by
the lists, several times pushed his whole head and chest beyond the
barriers. For which reason the Constable, Thomas of Woodstock,
claimed the horse swearing that he would have his head and chest,
namely however much of the horse had appeared inside the barrier;
whence the horse was adjudicated to him. But this was later; we
will revert to the form of the duel.

7.

Duels and royal politics in England 1388-99

In England during the last decades of the 14th century we have some striking examples of the use of judicial duels as part of politics among the high nobility. During the reign of Richard II, the young king was in constant competition with some of his uncles and cousins. When civil war actually broke out, the losers opened themselves up to accusations and prosecutions for treason. On a number of occasions, this meant trial by battle. In 1388, Nicholas Brembre, one of the King's partisans being tried by the King's enemies, demanded the right to defend himself by arms rather than face an ordinary court, which in cases of treason imposed savage punishments on those found guilty. He was refused; indeed, when the King tried to save Brembre, hostile members of Parliament threw their gauntlets before the King in defiance. Richard was in such an isolated position that he had to accept this provocative gesture and abandon his loyal supporters.

After a royal victory in 1397, two of the leading peers of the realm, both opponents of the King, Henry of Lancaster, Duke of Hereford and Thomas of Mowbray, Duke of Norfolk and Earl Marshal, accused each other of treasonous conversation. This conversation, which seems to have concerned the precariousness of their political standing, took place with no witnesses and so it was a classic example of a case where a judicial combat was needed to decide who was guilty of this insidious crime. King Richard allowed or even promoted a long preparatory period during which time the two peers could assemble the best armor available.

When the time came for the combat, King Richard prevented any fighting from taking place. The possible destruction of one of these peers was apparently too shocking an eventuality to contemplate. The Duke of Hereford was in fact a potential heir to King Richard, and one of the richest men in the Kingdom. On the day set for the duel, both the accused were sent into exile. Nevertheless this royal intervention did nothing to defuse an explosive political situation. In short order Hereford (Lancaster) returned from exile, deposed the King, claimed the throne and destroyed his opponents.

Henry's efforts to solidify his new regime led to the use of trial by battle, or at least its symbolism, to attack Richard's supporters. Henry's parliament, which was filled with his partisans, took up the question whether those who had cooperated with the deposed king in earlier civil conflicts could be held responsible for the deaths of those whom the King had executed. A scapegoat, the Earl of Aumale, was accused of treason and members of the House of Commons demanded that he be tried by combat. The new king was reluctant to use the duel, but found it difficult to rein in the bloodlust of his own followers, who were throwing around gages and making accusations with great freedom. This is a very striking example of the dangers and the attractions of trial by battle. What attracted was the definitive judgment supposedly promised by the duel. On the other hand, the use of such a procedure, which in cases of treason would end in somebody dying, stirred up passions and tended to undermine the authority of the normal courts and even of the King himself. The uncompromising logic of trial by battle could rip apart the solidarity of noble society. However, as attached noble warriors might have been to the right of self-help – a right that King Henry himself had appealed to, only weeks earlier, when invading England – it was in itself a threat to justice, or at least (in Henry's words) "law," and certainly order. Because trial by battle escalated conflicts, it often provoked extreme consequences, as Richard II had so recently had cause to learn. Overheated politics provided a justification for duels (consummated or not) between military men who accused one another of treason. Presumably this is what they were used to; this was the only kind of judgment that they respected, the one legal method that they could take part in without losing status.

Trial of Nicholas Brembre, England 1388. Thomas Favent,
The History ... of the Miraculous Parliament at Westminster—chronicle account

18. And on the 12th day of February, which was the first Monday of Lent, when the aforesaid Nicholas Brembre was made to appear, with certain articles proposed and read through before him, he requested a copy, and counsel, and a day for the sake of deliberating better how he would respond to them. And although what he sought was neither an equitable or customary thing, nay further against the rigor of the law, in so grave a criminal case we would have allowed the tiniest matter construably in his favor: had he begged in vain, it would have been imposed on him to answer the charges strictly. For it is read that he answered, "Whoever has charged me with these things, I give witness that I am present here ready to prove by battle with him in the arena that these same things are false." And Brembre said these things terrified that he would die in excruciating pain in the manner of traitors, and would prefer to expire as a knight fighting in arms than scandalously through the parliament's condemnation. Immediately the commemorated appellants with stern visage declared, "And we ourselves give witness and offer ourselves that we are ready to prove by battle with you in the arena that these same things are true." And they threw their gauntlets at

the King's feet; and at the same instant from everywhere in the place
flew gauntlets like snow from the other lords, knights, squires, and
commons, who declared in one voice, "And we pledge a duel for
proving on your head that the things said are true." Quicker than
speech the King departed for the day. And although these things
were not left unconsidered among the sleepers, nonetheless on the
next day, as an even heavier matter, appeared many of the crafts of
the city of London complaining about many injuries and extortions
torturously committed and carried forward against them elsewhere
by that same Nicholas Brembre. And since the crafts themselves
swore on their souls that they were not corrupted by hatred, fear,
or favor of anyone or any reward, nor were they declaring these
things maliciously but rather were accusing him concerning the
truth, Brembre then stood undone at last.

. . .

20. On the next day a sentence similar to that of the four condemned was given against Brembre, and when he was drawn from
the Tower through the city on a hurdle to Tyburn, resting at fur-
long intervals he gave great penance, beseeching mercy from God
and men against whom he had sinned in past times, and many
commiserating prayed for him. And when the noose was put on
him so that he might be hanged, the son of Northampton asked
him whether the aforesaid things done elsewhere to his father by
Brembre were legally done. For Northampton was formerly a mayor
of the city of London, a richer and more powerful citizen among
all those who were in the city, and through certain ones, associ-
ates who were death-bearing plagues, namely Brembre, Tresilian
and others, was enormously vexed by certain nefarious conspira-
cies and confederacies then condemned to death, and with all his
goods stripped hardly escaped alive. And concerning those things
Brembre confessed that neither piously nor justly but with a violent

heart for the sake of destroying Northampton he had infelicitously committed those things. And seeking forgiveness, hanging by the rope, he died when his throat was cut. Behold how good and pleasant it is to be raised up to honors! It seems to me better to carry out business at home among paupers than be thus lordly among kings, and at the end climb the ladder among thieves; since it is more a matter of onerousness than honor to assume the name of honor. You who are reading, look down to regard him, and you might be able to consider by their ends how their works receive results. For in every work be mindful of the end.

Hereford v. Norfolk, England 1398. *Chronicque de la traïson et mort de Richart deux roy Dengleterre* – chronicle account

And as the King was setting out on horseback to go to Shrewsbury, the Duke of Hereford came and presented a petition to the King, in which he impeached the Duke of Norfolk of treason, and challenged him to battle as a false and disloyal traitor to the realm of England. When the King had received the petition, he caused it to be read in the presence of the two lords, and then the Duke of Norfolk replied, that in all the Duke of Hereford wished to insinuate against him, he lied, false knight as he was. The King said to the Duke of Hereford, "Cousin Henry of Lancaster, the petition which I received from you has been here read, what say you before all present?" Upon which the Duke of Hereford removed his bonnet, which was black, from his head, and said, "My lord, as the petition which I have given you makes mention, so say I for troth, that Thomas of Mowbray, Duke of Norfolk, such as he is, is a traitor, false and recreant towards you and your royal majesty, to your crown, to the nobles, and to all the people of your realm." Then the

King asked the Duke of Norfolk, "What have you to say, Thomas?"
The Duke replied, "My dear sire, by your leave in answer to your
cousin, saving Your Grace, I say that Henry of Lancaster, Duke of
Hereford, has lied in that he has said and wished to insinuate against
me, like a false traitor and disloyal subject as he is." "Ho!" said the
King, "we have heard enough of that;" and he then commanded
the Duke of Surrey, who was then Marshal of England, to arrest
the two lords. It is true that the Duke of Lancaster, father of the
said Duke of Hereford, the Duke of York, the Duke of Albemarle,
Constable, and the Duke of Surrey, Marshal, these four princes were
bail, body for body, for the Duke of Hereford; and it was thought
that the Duke of Norfolk was not able to find bail, but was taken in
arrest to Windsor, and a guard was appointed over him until the
day that was appointed for the combat, and there he had master
armorers, as many as he pleased, to make his armor.

Item, when King Richard had returned from the Parliament of
Shrewsbury, in the year 1398, in the month of January, a day was appointed, within forty days, to hear at Windsor the two lords who had
accused each other of treason. (On the appointed day) King Richard
was seated on a platform which had been erected in the square of
the castle, and all the lords and prelates of his kingdom with him;
and there they caused to appear the Duke of Hereford, Earl Derby, appellant; and then the Duke of Norfolk, Earl Marshal, defendant, Then Sir John Bussy opened the proceedings on the part
of the King, saying "My lords, you know full well that the Duke
of Hereford has presented a petition to our sire the King, who is
here present in his seat of justice to administer right to those who
shall require it this day, as it becomes him and his royal office,"
And three days before was it proclaimed on behalf of the King that
none of the parties, on the one side or the other, should be so daring as to carry arms, on pain of being drawn and hung. And the

King caused the parties to he asked if they would not agree and make peace together, saying it would be much better. Accordingly, the Constable and the Marshal went, by the King's desire, and besought them to make up the matter and be reconciled, and that then the King would pardon all that they had said or done against him or his kingdom. But they both answered that never should peace be made between them. And when the King was told this, he commanded that they should be brought before him that he might hear what they had to say. Then a herald cried on the part of the King that the Duke of Hereford and the Duke of Norfolk should come forward before the King, to tell, each his reason, why they would not make peace together. And when they were come before the King and his counsel, the King said to them himself, "My lords, make matters up; it will be much better." "Saving your favour, my dear sovereign," said the Duke of Norfolk, "it cannot be, my honor is too deeply concerned." Then the King said to the Duke of Hereford, "Henry, say what it is you have to say to the Duke of Norfolk or, why you will not be reconciled." The Duke of Hereford had a knight, who, having asked and obtained permission from the King and the counsel to speak on behalf of the Duke, said, "Dear and sovereign lord, here is Henry of Lancaster, Duke of Hereford and Earl Derby, who declares, and I also for him, that Thomas, Duke of Norfolk, has received from you eight hundred thousand nobles to pay your men-at-arms who guard your city of Calais, whom he has not paid as he ought to have done . I say this is great treason, and calculated to cause the loss of your city of Calais: and I also say that he has been at the bottom of all the treasons committed in your kingdom these last eighteen years, and has, by his false counsel and malice, caused to be put to death my dear and beloved uncle, the Duke of Gloucester, son of King Edward, whom God absolve, and who was brother of my dearly beloved father the Duke of Lancaster, the Duke of Hereford says, and I on his part, that he will prove the truth of this by his body between any sunrise and sunset."

Then the King was wroth, and asked the Duke of Hereford if he acknowledged these as his words. To which he replied, "My dear lord, I do; and I also demand of you the right of wager of battle against him." Then the Duke of Norfolk's knight, who was very aged, demanded leave to speak; and when he had obtained leave, he began thus: "Most dread sovereign, behold here Thomas of Mowbray, Duke of Norfolk, who answers, and I for him, that with respect to all which Henry of Lancaster has said and shown, such as it is, Thomas of Mowbray, Duke of Norfolk, says, and I on his part, saving the reverence of yourself and your counsel, that it is all falsehood, and that he has lied falsely and wickedly like a false and disloyal knight; and that he has been more false and disloyal towards you, your crown, your royal majesty, and your kingdom, than he ever was, in intention or in deed. This will I prove, and defend myself as a loyal knight ought to do in encounter against him. I beseech you, and the counsel of your Majesty, that it may please you, in your kingly discretion, to consider and bear in mind what Henry of Lancaster, Duke of Hereford, such as he is, has said." Then the King asked the Duke of Norfolk if that was his speech, and if he wished to say anything more. The Duke of Norfolk, in person, answered the King: "My dear lord, it is true I have received so much gold from you to pay your people of your good city of Calais, which I have done. I say that the city of Calais is as well guarded and as much at your command now as it ever was, and also that no person of Calais has lodged any complaint to you against me. My dear and sovereign lord, for the journeys that I have performed in France on account of your noble marriage, and for the journey that the Duke of Albemarle and I took in Germany, where we expended much treasure, I never received from you either gold or silver. It is true, and I acknowledge, that I once laid an ambush to kill my lord of Lancaster, who is there seated; and it is true that my lord forgave me, and peace was made between us, for which I thank him. This is what I wish to say and to reply, and to support it I will defend myself against him. I beseech you to grant me justice, and trial of battle in tournament." The two parties were then withdrawn, and the King consulted with his counsel. Afterwards the two lords were summoned to hear the decision. Again the King desired them to be asked if they would be reconciled, or not. They both replied they would not; and the Duke of Hereford threw down his pledge, which the Duke of Norfolk received. Then swore the King by Saint John the Baptist that he would never more endeavor to reconcile those two; and Sir John Bussy, on the part of the King and counsel, announced that they should have trial of battle at Coventry, on a Monday in the month of August, and that there they should have their day and their lists.

Item. The Sunday next before the Monday appointed for the combat, arrived the lords who were about to fight in the city of Coventry. The same day, after dinner, went the Duke of Hereford, Earl Derby, to take leave of King Richard at a tower where he was lodging, which belonged to Sir William Bagot, and which was about a quarter of a league out of the city: and the following Monday, at break of day, went the Duke of Norfolk to take leave of the King, and thence went to the Carthusians to hear three masses, and afterwards rode to his tent, close to the lists, to have his armor put on; which was done by his esquire, Jacques Felm of Bohemia.

And the Duke of Hereford was armed in a beautiful house within the gate of the barrier of the city, which (house) had a handsome wooden pavilion near its gate, so placed that none could see within.

The Duke of Aumale, Constable, and the Duke of Surrey, Marshal, with their twenty followers, were all well-armed, and wore a livery of short doublets of red Kendal cloth full of belts, in the fashion of a silver girdle, upon each of which was written at length "Honniz soit celluy qui mal pense." [A variation of the famous motto "Evil to him who evil thinks."]

At eight o'clock, the Constable, the Marshal, and all the foreigners who had come from over sea, entered within the lists, as well as a Scotch knight, who was called Walter Stuart.

At nine o'clock the Duke of Hereford, the appellant, arrived in very noble array, with his followers, upon six noble chargers, well-armed and covered, and wearing his cognizance. And when he presented himself at the barrier of the lists, the Constable and the Marshal went forth to meet him, and asked him who he was, what he wanted, and for what purpose he was come thither. To whom he answered, " I am Henry of Lancaster, Duke of Hereford, and am come here to prosecute my appeal in combating Thomas Mowbray, Duke of Norfolk, who is a traitor, false and recreant to God, the King, his realm, and me."

Then the Constable and the Marshal administered to him the oath, and asked him if he would enter the lists on this point. He replied, he would; and placed forward his shield, which was argent, with a cross gules, like unto the arms of St. George. He then closed the visor of his helmet, signed himself with the sign of the cross with his hand as lightly as if he had not been armed, and called for his lance. The barrier was then opened, and he rode straight to his pavilion, which was covered with red roses, and, alighting from his charger, entered his pavilion, and awaited the coming of his adversary, as is the custom on such a day.

Afterwards Sir John Bussy came forward with a roll in his hand, which he read, and a herald proclaimed after him, "It is commanded by the King, by the Constable, and by the Marshal, that no person, poor or rich, be so daring as to put his hand upon the lists, on pain of having his hand chopped off; and that none enter within the lists, save those who have leave from the King and counsel, the Constable, and the Marshal, upon pain of being drawn and hung." And he cried on the part of the King, "Oez ! [= oyez] Behold here Henry of Lancaster, Duke of Hereford, appellant, who is come to the lists to do his duty against Thomas Mowbray, Duke of Norfolk, defendant; let him come in the lists to do his duty, upon pain of being declared false" which the herald cried thrice at each tribune of the lists.

As soon as proclamation had been made, the Constable and the Marshal went up to the Duke of Norfolk, who had made his appearance before the barrier of the lists, and administered to him the oath; and when he had been sworn, they opened the barrier, and he entered the lists, saying, "God speed the right!" then alighted before his pavilion, and hung his shield at his saddle-bow. Afterwards the Constable and the Marshal ordered the lances of the lords to be brought; and they measured them, to see if they were of the same length; and the Duke of Surrey handed the lance to the Duke of Hereford, and another knight gave the lance to the Duke of Norfolk. Then the herald cried, by order of the King, the Constable, and the Marshal, that they should take away the tents of the champions, that they should let go the chargers, and that each should perform his duty. When the Duke of Hereford had proved his lance, he pushed forward his shield, and signed himself with the sign of the cross; then placed his lance upon his thigh, and advanced seven or eight paces towards his adversary to perform his duty. The Duke of Norfolk remained motionless, and made no appearance of defense. Then the King rose up and cried, "Ho! ho!" and commanded that the Duke of Hereford's lance should be taken away, and that each should be conducted to his seat. There they remained nearly two hours after the battle was forbidden. At length the herald of Brittany mounted the tribune of the lists, whence he had before made proclamation, and cried on the part of the King, " Oez! " Then Sir John Bussy came forward, holding in his hand a large roll of writing, a full fathom long, and cried, "Oez! My lords, I inform you, by order of the King and council, the Constable, and the Marshal, that Henry of Lancaster, Duke of Hereford, appellant, and Thomas Mowbray, Duke of Norfolk, defendant, have both appeared here valiantly, and that each was, and is, ready to do his duty like a brave knight; but because the matters are so weighty between the two lords, it is decreed by the King and counsel, that Henry of Lancaster shall quit the realm for the term of ten years, and, if he return to the country before the ten years are passed, he shall be hung and beheaded." And when the proclamation was made, everyone had great marvel that the Duke of Hereford should be banished, inasmuch as he had performed his duty so gallantly; and they made so much noise that they could not hear each other speak, for everyone thought that he must have forfeited his honor. Presently a herald cried aloud, by the King's order, when they began to be more silent, "Hear the judgment of the King and counsel, it is as follows: That Thomas of Mowbray, Duke of Norfolk, shall quit the realm for the rest of his life, and shall choose whether he would dwell in Prussia, in Bohemia, or in Hungary, or would go right beyond sea to the land of the Saracens and unbelievers; that he shall never return to set foot again on Christian land; and that all his lands shall remain in the King's hands, to reimburse the money that he had received for the payment of the garrison of Calais, and misapplied; but that he shall be allowed ten thousand nobles a-year for his own use." After proclamation had been made, the Constable and the Marshal conducted the two lords sentenced to banishment before the King's tent, and the King forbade them ever to come into each other's presence, or to go where they would be likely to meet,

or to eat or drink in company, on pain of forfeiting their possessions. The King then caused the two lords to be sworn to obey his
commands, and afterwards they both mounted their horses and
immediately left the lists; and at parting the Duke of Norfolk said
to his people, "We might as well have gone to the great Parliament
at Shrewsbury, for if he and I had gone there, we should both have
been put to death, as the Earl of Arundel was." The morrow, King
Richard departed, and the Count of Saint Pol with him, for his
house at Leicester. As for the Duke of Surrey, he went with twenty
thousand men-at-arms to the war in Ireland, for the King. On the
Wednesday, the King arrived at Leicester, and there the two lords
who had been banished took their leave of him, ongoing abroad;
afterwards the King went to Windsor, and there the lords took their
final leave of the King, and also of the Queen.

A duel, then, could be dangerous to people who were not direct participants.
This is well illustrated by one of the most dramatic scenes to ever take place in
an English parliament, which occurred in October, 1399, early in the reign of
Henry IV. Henry, Duke of Lancaster and formerly Duke of Hereford, the accuser of Mowbray in the duel discussed above, had just deposed Richard II and
claimed the throne as his nearest male heir. Richard's supporters were few, but
the usurpation had made English politics tenser than ever. So many had been
accused and convicted of treason in the previous three years that no one knew
who might be next. When, therefore, Parliament began to investigate Richard's
secret murder of the Duke of Gloucester, the great lords all feared they might
be implicated. Attention to the role of the Duke of Aumale in that death led to
an accusation against him, then a near riot in the parliament hall:

Trouble in Parliament, England, October 1399. Thomas Favent, *the History of the Miraculous Parliament at Westminster* – chronicle account

Lord FitzWalter addressed the Duke of Aumale again: "You, Aumale, were the cause of the Duke of Gloucester's death. You were midwife to his murder. And this I shall prove by battle. There is my hood!" And so saying he threw down his hood, to which the Duke of Aumale responded with equal vehemence by throwing down his own hood. Seeing this, Lord Morley, Lord William de Beauchamp, the earl of Warwick himself, and nearly all the rest of the earls and barons also threw down their hoods to challenge Aumale on this point, whereupon there was such a mighty tumult and clamor from the commons [in parliament] offering battle on the same point that the King was afraid that the duke was about to be put to death before his very eyes. Rising therefore to restrain the lords, he first begged, then warned, and finally ordered them not to try to do anything which was against the law, but to act legally and only after proper discussion. Anything that might be done by any other means was as reprehensible as the crimes of those whom they were currently accusing. Impressed by this speech, the lords ceased their tumult.

This episode, like the earlier challenges made on Nicholas Brembre, says much about how the uncompromising logic of trial by battle could rip apart the solidarity of noble society. However attached noble warriors might have been to the right of self-help – a right that King Henry himself had appealed to, only weeks earlier, when invading England – it was in itself a threat to justice, or at least (in Henry's words above) "law," and certainly order. Because trial by battle took things to extremities it might provoke extreme consequences, as Richard II had so recently found out.

8.

Late deeds of arms as judicial duels

Although the 14th century saw the staging and recording of some of the best known judicial duels, their use slowly declined in the 15th century and beyond. If the use of these duels was rare, and took place in unusual circumstances, it nevertheless remained a possibility in various jurisdictions into the 16th century and even later. Duels might well have been as elaborate as they had ever been. In England the preparations for a duel could involve a number of governmental bodies, many skilled artisans, and considerable expense to the King:

Lyalton v. Norreys, England 1453. *Proceedings of the Privy Council* – legal documents (abbreviated and modernized):

31 Hen. VI. 1452-3.

11th May, 31 Hen. VI. 1453.—Memorandum, stating that on this day, in a Court holden at Whitehall by the lieutenant of the Constable of England, John Lyalton appealed Robert Norreys of high treason; that the 25th of the same month was appointed for them to do battle in Smithfield; that they should fight with glaive, short sword, dagger, and axe, instead of long sword; that counsel, who are named, were assigned to them; that it was therefore necessary that the sheriffs of London should be directed to gravel and sand the place, to erect a scaffold for the King, and to make lists and barriers for the battle; and that the serjeant of the King's armory should be commanded to provide armor and weapons for the combatants.

Between the eleventh and 25th May, 31 Hen. VI. 1453.—Petition to the King from John Lyalton, who had appealed Robert Norreys of treason, praying that letters of privy seal might be issued for carrying into effect the ordinances which had been made in the Court of the Constable of England (*Vide* the memorandum of the eleventh May).

On or about 23rd May, 31 Hen. VI. 1453—Minutes of the Council. The sheriffs of London to be directed to make a scaffold for the King, and lists and barriers, and to gravel and sand the ground in Smithfield; armor and weapons to be delivered by the Serjeant of the King's arms to John Lyalton, the appellant; and Thomas Bee, painter, to be one of his counsel.

23rd May, 31 Hen. VI. 1453—Letter from the King to Sir John Asteley, knight, and Thomas Montgomery, esquire, appointing them to be of counsel to John Lyalton, the appellant.

24th May, 31 Hen, VI. 1453.—Letter of similar import from the King to Thomas Bee, painter.

Ibid.—Letter from the King to Jenkyn Stanley, Serjeant of arms, commanding him to deliver arms and weapons to the appellant.

Ibid.—Writ to the Sheriffs of London, commanding them to prepare barriers and lists in West Smithfield, to have the same well graveled and sanded, and also to erect a scaffold. 29th May, 31 Hen.VI. 1453.—Petition to the King from John Lyalton, the appellant, praying for a grant of money to enable him to purchase necessaries for the ensuing battle, and that Clampard the smith might be commanded to deliver weapons to him: —Five marks were granted to him.

22nd June, 31 Hen. VI. 1453.—Petition to the King from Robert Norreys, the defendant, to the same effect (*mutatis mutandis*) as that from Lyalton, the appellant, dated between the eleventh and 25th of May.

Ibid.—Letter from the King to Sir Hugh John and others, appointing them to be of counsel to Robert Norreys, the defendant.

Ibid.—Memorandum containing the names of those who were appointed to be of counsel to the appellant and defendant in the above-mentioned appeal.

23rd June, 31 Hen. VI. 1453.—Petition to the King from John Lyalton, the appellant, praying for a tent or pavilion for the day of battle, and that Clampard the smith might be commanded to deliver to him such weapons as were necessary .

In the early 15th century, there was still a particular interest in the legal, ritual, and practical structure of judicial duels. We have seen that in the 1430s, Johan Hyll (Hill), an armorer in the service of the King of England, found it worthwhile to write an entire treatise in great detail about how such a duel might be staged.

Although he was particularly interested in the special armor that combatants might use to survive such a dangerous undertaking he gave attention to every aspect. It is also worth noticing that Hyll believed that some kind of duel was among the most worshipful exercises in arms that a warrior can undertake. This treatise once again shows us that a judicial combat involving men of high rank and enjoying the particular attention of the King was elaborate and expensive. (Note the arrangements made to prepare the field for a combat between Lyalton v. Norreys in England in 1453, and to prepare painted weapons and heraldic paraphernalia for the Astley-Boyle duel of 1442.) We are not surprised to find that ordinary crimes committed by ordinary people seldom resulted in a judicial combat, and if a judicial combat was called for in such a case, it was often resolved by a ruling by a judge instead of actual combat.

Preparations for the Astley-Boyle duel England, 1442 – government documents

[For the Astley-Boyle combat of 1442, a painter was directed to provide the following:]

The Paynter.
Also one Trappowr of his armes, [horse trapper, caparison]
Also one Trappoure of his device,
Also iij coates of Armes,
Also vj scochens of his Armes, [escutcheons]
Also one phane of his armes for his coate, [banner]
Also one pencell beten, to bere in his hande, [pennoncel]
[beten = embroidered]
Also one pencell beaten of his devise,
Also one castinge speare payntd.]

Newithon v. Hamilton, Scotland, 1548, Raphael Holinshed *Chronicles of England, Scotland, and Ireland*

The eight and twentieth of May, his lordship won the castle of Yester, after he had beaten it right sore with terrible battery of cannon shot for the time it lasted, and therewith having made a reasonable breach for the soldiers to enter, they within yielded with condition to have their lives saved: which the Lord Grebe was contented to grant to them all, one only excepted, who during the siege uttered unseemly words of the King, abusing his majesty's name with vile and most opprobrious terms. They all coming forth of the castell in their shirts, humbled themselves to my lord Grey (as became them) and upon strait examination who should be the railer that was excepted out of the pardon, it was known to be one Newithon a Scot: but he to save himself, put it to one Hamilton, and so these two gentlemen accusing one another, the truth could not be decided otherwise than by a combat, which they required, and my lord Grey thereunto assented, and pronounced judgment so to have it tried: which he did the rather, because all men doo seemed resolute in the trial of truth (as in a very good cause) by loss of life to gain an endless name; as one smith:

Mors spernenda viris vt fama perennis alatur. (Death is scorned by men so that eternal fame should be nourished.)

At the appointed time they entered the lists, set up for that purpose in the market place of Hadington, without other apparel saving their doublets and hosen, weaponed with sword, buckler and dagger. At the first entry into the lists, Hamilton kneeling down, made his hearty prayer to God, that it might please him to gigue victory unto the truth, with solemn protestation that he never uttered any such words of King Edward of England, as his adversary charged him with. On the other side Newithon being troubled (as it seemed) with his false accusation, argued unto the beholders his guilty conscience. Now were the sticklers in a readiness, and the combaters with their weapons drawn fell to it, so that betwixt them were striken six or seven blows right lustily. But Hamilton being very fierce and eager, upon trust of his innocence, constrained Newithon to gigue ground almost to the end of the lists; and if he had driven him to the end in deed, then by the law of arms he had won the victory. Newithon perceiving himself to be almost at point to be thus overcome, stepped forwards again, and gave Hamilton such a gash on the leg, that he was not able longer to stand, but fell therewith down to the ground, and then Newithon falling on him, incontinently slue him with a dagger.

There were gentlemen present that knowing as they took it for certain, how Newithon was the offender (although fortune had favored him in the combat) would gladly have ventured their lives against him man for man, if it might have been granted: but he challenging the law of arms, had it granted by my lord Grey, who gave him also his own gown beside his own back, and a chain of gold which he then ware. Thus was he well rewarded how so ever he deserved:. but he escaped not so, for afterwards as he was riding betwixt the borders of both the realms, he was slain and cut in pieces.

Legal records continue to reveal occasional resort to established procedures (such as Philip IV's ordinance in France) and in England the old use of combat in cases involving the writ of right (disputes over land) was still theoretically possible. Yet professional lawyers and judges and their lords slowly abandoned judicial combats as a possibility. In France, where several legal compilations were issued during the 16th century, the codifiers took the opportunity to limit trial by battle until, in 1599, they were abolished. In England, trial by battle survived as a possibility into the early 19th century, mainly because it was never used after the 15th century. When, in 1817 and 1819, accused murderers demanded that they be allowed to defend themselves in trials, the laws abolishing trial by battle were passed in a single night's session of Parliament.

Clerics and legal authorities had been opposed to trial by battle for a long time and did their best to eliminate a practice that they felt was illogical and (in some contexts) blasphemous , but the belief of gentlemen in their right defend themselves through self-help (or "war") not only survived but revived very strongly in the 16th century. In this era, duels of honor took place not because a specific legal issue had to be decided, but because one gentleman had impugned the honor of another. (Examples: Glarains and the *Song of My Cid*). It is quite possible that the confrontation began with one man accusing another of a crime, but the justification for a duel came when the accused gentleman rebuked the accuser as a liar. Then the issue became one of deciding which of the two was truthful and honorable. This is similar to the logic of ordeals (and "ordeals by public opinion" in the early Middle Ages). Gentlemen fought duels because they wished, in the face of a malicious attack, to maintain their standing in society.

Such duels of honor were in fact illegal in the later Middle Ages and after. They became commonplace in some areas of Europe at certain times when the legal courts had lost their ability to prosecute and punish crimes, especially when the crimes were committed by gentlemen. During the 16th century, Italy, with its fragmented and complex political environment, became one of the first places in which duels of honor became commonplace. The practice spread to France, despite the long-established official discouragement of duels. The French religious civil wars in the 16th century (there were nine of them!) led to such turmoil that it became practically obligatory for gentlemen who were accused of crimes or even just insulted to take part in a deadly confrontation to settle the matter, the matter being specifically the claim that another man was not to be trusted or valued as a gentleman. Gentlemen were still assumed to be warriors, whether or not they actually were. Thus, they had both the right and the obligation to uphold family and personal honor. Even though many, perhaps most, nobles accepted—or at least did not reject—that assumption, dueling in this last era was socially accepted but legally frowned upon and in fact, duelists were prosecuted for killing their opponents. There are many requests for pardons in the French archives in which such killers presented the circumstances of the duel and the death they had caused, and even though these pardon requests reflect the point of view of the survivor, it is clear enough that much of what has been labeled as dueling was murder by ambush.

Duels of honor took place when and where the status of "gentleman" still was connected to the concept of a special military caste. It is worth remembering that medieval gentlemen were all, in theory, members of the military order of society, even if they were not necessarily nobles. It is worth noting that a new society with a strong identification with republican virtue, the United States in the Early Republic period, also generated a quasi-official Order of the Cincinnati, made up of veterans of the Revolution, members who were recognizably gentlemen by European standards, and some of them, including many of the most prominent, took part in dueling. Aaron Burr, the third vice president, shot and killed the first secretary of the treasury, Alexander Hamilton. Andrew Jackson, though he came from an undistinguished family, was a great hero of the War of 1812 and later wars against the Native Americans; his numerous duels to defend his wife's good name may have been one of his stronger claims to gentility.

But in the course of the 19th century, the association between the status of gentleman and the usually hereditary status of professional warrior weakened. Duels of honor became a rather eccentric practice, with no association with military or social life. For instance, student fencing clubs at universities in continental Europe existed, but they were obviously anachronistic displays of romantic young men. They were not connected in any way to medieval or early modern ways of asserting one's status. Duels are best seen as deeds of arms, and deeds of arms as a central demonstration of noble or gentle status were long obsolete when Andrew Jackson fought for his wife or Heidelberg students created the new custom of fighting to acquire scars.

William L. (Will) McLean IV

March 23, 1957 - October 24, 2015

Graduate of the College of Art, Architecture and Planning, Cornell University

Married Wendy Whiteman, 1982; they had two daughters and one grandchild.

At the time of his death, Will was President and Chairman of Independent Publications, Inc., a newspaper holding company.

A member of La Belle Compagnie, a living history group portraying a noble household in the days of the Hundred Years War, and of the Society for Creative Anachronism.

Acknowledgements

Many people have made it easier to write this book. The first who should be thanked is Ariella Elema, who early on generously discussed with me her related work in her prize-winning dissertation. I look forward to a fuller treatment of trial by battle from her. Freelance Academy Press, particularly Greg Mele, Christian Tobler, and Bob Charrette have been very supportive, both of this book and of the Deeds of Arms series as a whole.

My challenge was to decipher source material in medieval French and German. Among the people who helped me untangle sentences and translate obscure vocabulary were Tracie Brown, Steve Boyd (Andrixos), Christos Nussli (many thanks to you!), Tasha Kelly, Kathy Krause, and my long-time collaborator Phil Paine. Matthew Bailey's very recent *Song of My Cid* and Richard Barton's translated monastic charters have not helped just me but have provided scholars in many places with permanent resources.

Abbreviated References

Johnes -- Jean Froissart. *Chronicles,* trans. Thomas Johnes. 2 vols. London, 1862

KL -- Jean Froissart, *Oeuvres,* ed. Kervyn de Lettenhove. 25 vols. (Brussels, 1867-77).

Source Index

The source excerpts that make up much of the book are listed here in such a way as to make them as easy as possible to find. In this index, each source is identified by (1) a short version of the title used in the main body of the book, (2) a URL that will lead the reader to an online version of the source, where such exists , and (3) a standard bibliographical listing.

An early medieval duel

http://sourcebooks.fordham.edu/basis/gregory-hist.asp#book10

History of the Franks by Gregory Bishop of Tours. Translated by Ernest Brehaut. New York: Columbia University Press, 1916.

Abbots Daibert and Otbrannus prevent a battle between their monks

http://www.uncg.edu/~rebarton/judicialduels.htm#duel2

Chauvin, Yves, ed. *Cartulaire de l'abbaye de Saint-Serge,* 2 vols. Translated by Richard Barton. Memoire dactylographie soutenu devant la Faculté des Lettres de Caen (1969), vol. 1, no. 216, pp. 263-265.

Trouble between two monasteries leads to a judicial duel

http://www.uncg.edu/~rebarton/judicialduels.htm#duel3

Marchegay, Paul. "Duel judiciaire entre des communautes religieuses, 1098," *Bibliotheque de l'Ecole des Chartes*, 1 (1839-1840), 552-564. Translated by Richard Barton.

Song of My Cid

http://miocid.wlu.edu/index2.php?v=eng

Bailey, Matthew, ed. *Cantar de Mio Cid*. Translated by Matthew Bailey. Austin: University of Texas, 2017. miocid.wlu.edu.

Canon 18 of the 4th Lateran Council

http://sourcebooks.fordham.edu/halsall/basis/lateran4.asp

Schroeder, H. J. *Disciplinary Decrees of the General Councils: Text, Translation and Commentary*. St. Louis: B. Herder, 1937, 236-296.

Honoré Bouvet, *Tree of Battles*

The tree of battles of Honoré Bonet (sic). Translated/introduced by G.W. Coopland. Liverpool: University Press, 1949.

Ordinance of Philip IV

http://tinyurl.com/hkpanwo

Ceremonies des gages de Bataille …du bon roi Philippe de France. Paris: Crapelet, 1830. Translated by Steven Muhlberger.

Duke of Gloucester's Ordinance

Dillon, "On a MS Collection of Ordinances of Chivalry of the Fifteenth Century, Belonging to Lord Hastings," *Archaeologia*, LVII (1902), 62-66.

Guyenne Ordinance, thirteenth—fourteenth century

http://gallica.bnf.fr/ark:/12148/bpt6k102538b/f107.image

"Formalités des duels et combats judiciaires en Guyenne dans les XIIIe ou XIVe siècles" in *Bulletin Trimestriel de la Société de Borda*. Translated to modern French by L. Lacouture , and to English by Steven Muhlberger. 38 (1914): 73-87.

Johan Hyll (Hill), *Treatise of the Points of Worship in Arms*, England, 1443

Dillon, "On a MS Collection of Ordinances of Chivalry of the Fifteenth Century, Belonging to Lord Hastings," *Archaeologia*, LVII (1902), 62-66. Modernized by Steven Muhlberger.

Theobald Giss v. Seitz von Althaim

http://tinyurl.com/znwj5ou

Mair, Paul Hector. *De arte athletica II* - BSB Cod.icon. 393(2, Augsburg, Mitte 16. Vol 6Jh. [BSB-Hss Cod.icon. 393(2)]. Translated by Steven Muhlberger.

Glairains v. Montravel, France, 1375 (1429)

http://gallica.bnf.fr/ark:/12148/bpt6k112212p?rk=42918;4

Chazaud A.-M., ed. *La chronique du bon duc Loys de Bourbon*. Translated by Steven Muhlberger. Paris: Librairie Renouard, 1876.

Carrouges v. Le Gris

https://faculty.nipissingu.ca/muhlberger/FROISSART/TRIAL.HTM

Bellaguet M.L., ed. *Chronique du Religieux de Saint-Denys*. v. 1.Paris: Crapelet, 1839.

Extract of the registers of the parlement of Paris -- legal documents

KL 12: 368-71. Translated by Steven Muhlberger.

Jean le Coq, Note concerning the duel of Jacques le Gris

KL 12: 366-8. Translated by Steven Muhlberger.

Annesley v. Katrington

Riley, Henry Thomas, ed. *Thomas Walsingham, quondam monachi S. Albani, Historia anglicana.* . London: Longman, Green, Longman, Roberts, and Green. 2 vols. 1863-4. Translated by Steven Muhlberger

Trial of Nicholas Brembre (chronicle of Thomas Favent)

http://falcon.arts.cornell.edu/prh3/310/texts%5Cfavent.html

Favent, Thomas. *the History or Narration Concerning the Manner and Form of the Miraculous Parliament at Westminster,* trans. Andrew Galloway. In: Steiner, Emily and Candace Barrington. *The Letter of the Law: Legal Practice and Literary Production in Medieval England.* Ithaca, New York, and London: Cornell Univ. Press, 2002, pp.231-52.

Hereford v. Norfolk

http://gallica.bnf.fr/ark:/12148/bpt6k5440677p

Williams, Benjamin. *Chronicque de la traïson et mort de Richart deux roy Dengleterre* , mise en lumière d'après un manuscrit de la bibliothèque royale de Paris. London: aux dépens de la Société, 1846.

Trouble in Parliament (chronicle of Thomas Favent)

http://prh3.arts.cornell.edu/310/texts/favent.html

Favent, Thomas. *The History or Narration Concerning the Manner and Form of the Miraculous Parliament at Westminster.* Translated by Andrew Galloway. In: Steiner, Emily and Candace Barrington. *The Letter of the Law: Legal Practice and Literary Production in Medieval England.* Ithaca, New York, and London: Cornell Univ. Press, 2002, pp.231-52.

Lyalton v. Norreys

http://tinyurl.com/jmh7ywl

England, and Harris Nicolas. 1834. *Proceedings and ordinances of the Privy Council of England*. London: Printed by G. Eyre and A. Spottiswoode. Vol 6 pp. 129, 132-39. (31 Hen VI 1452-3) Abbreviated and modernized by Will McLean.

Astley v Boyle 1442. Pierpont Morgan Library, 775.

Newithon v. Hamilton

https://willscommonplacebook.blogspot.ca/2010/02/newton-and-hamilton-scottish-gentlemen.html?m=0.

http://english.nsms.ox.ac.uk/holinshed/texts.php?text1=1587_8128

Holinshed, Raphael. *Chronicles of England, Scotland, and Ireland*. London: 1587, Volume 6, pp. 992-993.

Bibliography

Will McLean's works

A Commonplace Book: Deeds of Arms and other matters medieval and otherwise. (blog) http://willscommonplacebook.blogspot.com/

"Outrance and Plaisance," *Journal of Medieval Military History,* 8 (2010): 155-70.

(as Galleron de Cressy) **"Running a Tournament by King René's Rules"** *Tournaments Illuminated.* Issue #108, Fall 1993.

(as Galleron de Cressy) "A New Way to Get Maimed" *Tournaments Illuminated.* Issue #112, Fall 1994.

(with Jeffrey L. Forgeng) *Daily Life in Chaucer's England.* Westport, CT.: Greenwood Press, 1995.

(Obituary at Legacy.com) http://www.legacy.com/obituaries/dailylocal/obituary. aspx?pid=176242444

Other books and articles

Bartlett, Robert. *Trial by Fire and Water: The Medieval Judicial Ordeal.* Oxford: Clarendon, 1986.

Billacois, François. *The Duel: Its Rise and Fall in Early Modern France.* Edited and translated by Trista Selous. New Haven, CT: Yale University Press, 1990.

Elema, Ariella. *Trial by Battle in France and England.* PhD dissertation. University of Toronto, 2012.

Muhlberger, Steven. *Deeds of Arms: Formal Combats in the Late Fourteenth Century.* Highland Village, TX: Chivalry Bookshelf, 2005.

Rogers, Clifford. *The Wars of Edward III: Sources and Interpretations.* Woodbridge: Boydell Press, 2000.

Glossary

avantbras Plate armor to protect the forearm.

bascinet A light helmet shaped close to the head, either open-faced or visored.

caleçons Drawers or underpants.

camail A chainmail drape that hangs from a helmet and protects the head and shoulders

chausses Leg (thigh) armor.

false lists List barriers outside of the "principal lists." The combat took place within the area enclosed by the principal lists, while officials who observed and regulated the combat often did so in the space between the false and principal lists.

jupon A close-fitting padded garment worn over armor.

Noble A gold coin.

parlement, parliament Originally, any kind of assembly. The French term parlement came to designate important regional courts (especially the Parlement of Paris), while the English parliament was an early form of the representative bodies of today.

pavise A large oblong shield used by infantry to cover the entire body.

pledge [of battle] A legal procedure involving judicial combat. Also an object used to symbolize a commitment to a pledge of battle.

pourpoint A quilted doublet.

noon, nones In various contexts, either today's noon (midday) or the ninth hour after sunrise (roughly 3 p.m.)

prudomme A man noted for his excellence: in goodness, wisdom, trustworthiness; or in some skill, such as military prowess.

rerebras A piece of plate armor for the upper arm.

sabatons Metal shoes that armored the top of the foot.

Te igitur The first two words of the "canon" of the mass, designating a short prayer very familiar to medieval Catholics.

voider A mail gusset that covers areas not covered by plate armor.

weir A low dam or underwater barrier that raises the level of a river.